HYGGE

How To Hygge Without Buying Into The Hype

By Elizabeth Jones

© **Copyright 2020 by Elizabeth Jones** - All rights reserved.

This document is geared towards providing exact and reliable information in regard to the topic and issue covered. The publication is sold with the idea that the publisher is not required to render accounting, officially permitted or otherwise qualified services. If advice is necessary, legal or professional, a practiced individual in the profession should be ordered.

- From a Declaration of Principles which was accepted and approved equally by a Committee of the American Bar Association and a Committee of Publishers and Associations.

In no way is it legal to reproduce, duplicate, or transmit any part of this document in either electronic means or in printed format. Recording of this publication is strictly prohibited, and any storage of this document is not allowed unless with written permission from the publisher. All rights reserved.

The information provided herein is stated to be truthful and consistent, in that any liability, in terms of inattention or otherwise, by any usage or abuse of any policies, processes, or directions contained within is the solitary and utter responsibility of the recipient reader. Under no circumstances will any legal responsibility or blame be held against the publisher for any reparation, damages, or monetary loss due to the information herein, either directly or indirectly.

Respective authors own all copyrights not held by the publisher.

The information herein is offered for informational purposes solely and is universal as so. The presentation of the information is without a contract or any type of guarantee assurance.

The trademarks that are used are without any consent, and the publication of the trademark is without permission or backing by the trademark owner. All trademarks and brands within this book are for clarifying purposes only and are owned by the owners themselves, not affiliated with this document.

Table of Contents

Introduction	4
Chapter One: What is Hygge?	6
Chapter Three: Using Hygge in Your Life	16
Chapter Four: Embracing Hygge at Work	31
Chapter Five: How to Make Your Garden Hygge	43
Chapter Six: Some Tips to Follow Hygge	60
Conclusion	81
Resources	83

Introduction

Over the last few years, you may have heard a lot about Hygge. It's a word that most people struggle to pronounce. It's difficult to explain what this word means since there is no literal translation for this word. It's more of an emotion or feeling. The objective is to create intimacy, finding pleasure in the smaller things, and connecting you with the people you love.

The Hygge lifestyle is about being mindful of what you do and living in the present moment. You can adopt this lifestyle in many ways, and this lifestyle is said to be the happiest lifestyle on Earth. Do not make the mistake of looking at this as a trend. All you need to do is to make simple changes to your lifestyle.

The introduction sets the stage for the entire book, creating a bridge between the reader and the concept of hygge. It aims to captivate the audience's interest and provide a glimpse into what the book will explore.

Discuss the increasing popularity of hygge beyond Denmark and its emergence as a lifestyle trend embraced worldwide. Share a personal anecdote or experience that led you to explore and appreciate hygge. This creates a relatable connection between the author and the reader.

Clearly articulate the purpose of the book, whether it's to inform, inspire, or guide readers in incorporating hygge into their lives. Provide a brief overview of the chapters and themes that the book will explore, creating anticipation and setting expectations for what the reader will gain. Extend an invitation to the reader to embark on a journey of comfort, connection, and well-being.

Encourage an open mind and a willingness to explore the principles of hygge. Highlight the importance of hygge in today's fast-paced world, emphasizing its potential to bring balance, joy, and a sense of fulfillment. Recognize that everyone's journey with hygge will be unique, and the book is a guide rather than a rulebook, encouraging readers to tailor hygge to their individual lifestyles.

In this book, I will provide you all the information you need to know about Hygge. You'll learn how you can incorporate Hygge into your house and life. And I will provide you with tips to help you make the transition from clutter and stress to Hygge, with ease. Enjoy your journey!

Chapter One: What is Hygge?

An Introduction to Hygge

You may have heard of the word 'Hygge' quite often over the last few years, especially during winter. Let me try to explain what this term means. According to Google, Hygge is a quality of comfortable conviviality and coziness that makes people feel content and happy. It also aids in maintaining the physical and mental wellbeing of people. This is the foundation of the Danish culture. The word Hygge is pronounced as "Hoo-ga." In simple words, this Danish word encompasses the feeling of coziness with a lifestyle that improves your physical and mental wellbeing. It also ensures that you learn to cherish the simple things in life.

Ever enjoyed reading a book on rainy days or a hot cup of cocoa on a cold winter's day, then you have experienced 'Hygge.' Meik Wiking is the CEO of an institute known as the Happiness Research Institute in Denmark. According to Meik, 'Hygge' is an important part of being Danish. It is a defining feature of their cultural identity. Some might even consider it an integral part of their DNA.

In the book 'The Little Book of Hygge' Wiking says, "What freedom is to Americans, Hygge is to Danes." This nationwide obsession with all things cozy is the reason why the Danish are the happiest people in the world, despite the harsh cold winters they experience. In recent years, the rest of the world has started to catch up on this wonderful lifestyle or way of living.

Hygge is a Danish term that encapsulates a feeling of comfort, coziness, and contentment. This subchapter serves as a foundational overview of what hygge is and its cultural significance.

Explore the essential components that contribute to hygge, including warmth, connection, and an appreciation for simple pleasures. Delve into the cultural roots of hygge, tracing its origins in Danish culture and understanding how it has become a fundamental aspect of Danish lifestyle. Offer linguistic insights into the term itself, explaining its pronunciation ("hoo-gah") and linguistic nuances. Provide examples of how hygge manifests in everyday activities, from enjoying a cup of tea to creating a cozy reading nook. Discuss how the concept of hygge has gained global popularity and why people from various cultures find it appealing. Address the distinction between hygge and the pursuit of happiness, emphasizing that hygge is more about enjoying the journey than reaching a destination. Include relevant quotes or insights from experts, authors, or individuals who have embraced hygge as a way of life.

History

The Germans have a concept called gemütlichkeit. The idea of Hygge that the Danish follow is quite similar to that. Gezelligheid is a cozy and warm lifestyle that the German people follow. This culture is one that the Danes have followed since the early 1800s. This term was derived from the Norwegian word that means wellbeing.

The Danish use the word 'Hygge' as both an adjective and noun, but this is not just a term in their language. It is a way of life. It was only in 2016 that the UK caught up with this type of lifestyle after numerous articles and books were published about this way of life. Hygge became very popular, and it was even added as one of the words of the year in the Collins list in the year 2016. This word came second to Brexit.

The United States went gaga over the term Hygge in the year 2017, and the people did their best 'The New Yorker' and 'The New York Times' explained the concept quite well, and close to eight books were published in a few months that popularized the word. This word also began to trend on social media. By the end of 2016, close to 30% of the homes in the United States followed this lifestyle. Pinterest named this lifestyle as the hottest trend. Over 4 million posts on Pinterest and Instagram were tagged with the hashtag '#Hygge.' Many users have also taken to Twitter to talk about Hygge.

What Should You Consider Hygge?

Some may ask if wearing sweatpants and sitting on the couch counts as Hygge. Well, yes, it does. Hyggebukser is what the Danes call sweatpants. You would never be caught dead wearing these pants in public, would you? You will only wear them at home while reading a book or watching your favorite show. The Danes love coming up with different names, and they have added the word 'Hygge' to other words. Some examples are:
- Hyggelig: This means Hygge-like
- Hyggekrog: This indicates a place in your house where you can get comfortable or cozy

When you wrap yourself up in a blanket and stare out of a window looking at people walk by you, are following the Hygge lifestyle. Here are some examples of how to Hygge.
Candles
Danes believe that candles are the best way to create a Hyggelig atmosphere in your house. According to the Wiking, the Danes burn close to 15 pounds of candle wax every year. This is more than any other country does. All you need to do is turn the lights off and light some candles up.
Fireplace

There is nothing cozier and better than curling up by the fireplace on a cold winter's night. This setting will be better, especially if you have decorated the mantel for winter.

Throw Blankets

Regardless of whether you use a heated throw, a thick blanket, or a chunky knit, it is always a good idea to have something to wrap around yourself. You can also use the sweater that your grandmother knitted for you, an oversized pair of socks or sweaters if you want to follow the Hygge lifestyle.

Hot Drinks, Homemade Sweets, and Comfort Food

You must eat the right food if you want to create a Hyggelig atmosphere at home. When you have a nice fire going, or you have decorated the place with candles, you do not want to spend money on an expensive meal in a restaurant. Remember, Hygge is about comfort and familiarity.

In Denmark, this can mean meatballs, hot chocolate, hot coffee, pastries, and other foods. However, it is very different in the United States. You can choose to cook your favorite dish, spend the weekend baking, or simply drink something nice and warm. Winter is indeed the time for everything that is Hygge, but the Danes practice this lifestyle throughout the year. If you want to follow Hygge during the summer, you can have backyard dinners, outdoor movie nights, and bonfires on the beach or picnics.

What Hygge is What it is Not

Using Your Phone

This is one of the worst things to do, especially if you want to follow the Hygge lifestyle. You can watch TV if you like, but it is better if you invite a few friends over for a good movie. You must build and maintain relationships with your friends and family if you want to follow this lifestyle.

Hibernating Through the Winter

You must get off the couch and take a long walk. This is an especially good thing to do in winter. You do not always have to stay indoors, reading a book, and drinking a nice cup of hot coffee or chocolate by the fireplace. Make sure that you appreciate nature as well.

Hard Rules

The book 'The Life-Changing Magic of Tidying Up' written by Marie Kondo, went on to become the bestseller in 2014. This book talks about decluttering your home and keeping only those things that add "sparkle" to life. This may seem hard now, but the 'Hygge' lifestyle is more forgiving and friendlier to adapt. You must understand that Hygge is everything simple. This lifestyle encourages people to learn to live a little. Now, you know why so many people around you have started to follow this lifestyle.

Following the Trend

This lifestyle or practice is more about creating your atmosphere or environment with those things that you need. You are doing the opposite if you only want to buy expensive stuff. The world has started to wonder if the UK and the American versions of 'Hygge' are just ways for companies to sell their products to maximize their profits. You can read more about this in the article "The Hygge Conspiracy," written in the Guardian. You may now wonder how you can follow this lifestyle without falling for this hype. This book will help you gather all the information there is about Hygge. It will help you appreciate the simplest things in life that will bring you joy.

During the winter, don't complain about the weather. Just light up some candles, make a hot drink, pick up a book you've been reading or turn on the TV, roll up in a blanket, and just sink into the coziness. If you feel social, cook up your favorite recipe, invite some friends over for a movie, or a game night. Have fun and get 'Hygge' with it!

Chapter Two: Benefits of Hygge

Now that you know the basics of Hygge, let us look at some benefits of this lifestyle.

Emotional Benefits
The Hygge décor will promote a sense of peace and calm in your living space. When you make sense of your environment and experiences through the use of sound, taste, touch, smell, and sight, it does not come as a surprise that you will be less anxious. You will create a cozy space that will promote emotional safety and wellbeing. These feelings of safety and comfort will allow you to let your guard down. This will help you be more present, and you will be open to connecting with the people around you. Some examples of Hygge are:
- Lower stress
- Increased feelings of self-worth
- Less anxiety
- Less depression
- Increased optimism
- Practicing gratitude
- Improving self-compassion
- A sense of mindfulness

Mindful Eating
Food is a very big part of your life, and more so when it comes to socializing. If you choose to follow the Hygge lifestyle, you need to choose those foods that are hyggelig.

The same goes for the cooking and preparing process, too. Regardless of whether you cook for your friends and family or only for yourself, Hygge will encourage you to take care of your body in the best way.

You will learn to feed yourself the best food possible. You must understand that the Hygge lifestyle does not restrict you from eating the food you love.

You should go ahead and eat a piece of cake if you feel like it. But you need to make sure that you enjoy every bite of the cake. Food is an important aspect to consider if you want to improve your physical and mental wellbeing. All you need to do is learn to enjoy every morsel. Make sure you indulge your taste buds. When you follow this approach to eating, you will learn to eat whole and quality foods. You can make a huge pot of homemade soup and share a bowl of soup with your friends and family.

A Calm Mind

When you follow the Hygge lifestyle, you are expected to slow down. You must enjoy the present and every moment. Everybody is a part of the rat race, and people are always going since they do cannot do anything else. You must understand that it is not healthy to rush. It is not good for your mind or body. You must learn to pause or switch off. Do nothing. Doing nothing is as good as performing any Hyggelig activity. One of the easiest ways to calm your mind after a long day at work is to turn off your electronics and enjoy a nice bath. Instead of sitting in front of the television, light up some candles and set the mood in your bathroom. You can use any essential oil that you like, but lavender is the best since it helps to soothe your mind. You can then moisturize your skin with coconut oil. Now, sip some chamomile tea, grab a good book, and get cozy in your bed.

Physical Benefits

When you feel calm and safe, your body will also respond in the right way. When your body perceives any danger or threat, it will naturally switch into a response of freeze, fight, or flight. A hygge-style environment will create an atmosphere of comfort and safety. It is only when you do this that you will feel more relaxed. It is in spaces like these that you will no longer need to scan your environment or atmosphere for any threats. Some examples of the physical benefits are:

- Better sleep
- Weight loss and regulation
- Lower cortisol spikes
- Reduced usage of alcohol and other substances
- Practicing self-care

Relaxed Muscles

A hot bath with bath salts and essential oils will relax your muscles. People do not know how tensed or stressed they are. They do not know how tight the muscles in their shoulders are. When you are in a bath, and you focus only on calming your mind and body, you can unwind yourself. A hot bath can heal you in miraculous ways.

The Best Sleep

If you want to have a Hygge ritual every evening and want to prioritize sleep, you can do that too. You will see that your sleep will have improved ever since you started following this lifestyle. When you dedicate some time to yourself every evening to relax, you will sleep much better. Make sure that you switch all your screens off. Make yourself some hot tea, read a few pages, lie in your bed next to your partner, or go through some photos in your album. This will set you up for the best sleep you have ever had, and you will wake up rejuvenated and rested the next morning.

Social Benefits

When you feel emotionally safe and comfortable, you will be likely to nurture your relationships with other people. When you follow a Hygge lifestyle, you will need to connect with loved ones, friends, and family. When you spend time with the people you love, you will develop a better relationship with them. Research shows that it is these relationships that will impact your wellbeing and health. People are more confident when they connect with other people. You will be comfortable with taking risks and will allow yourself to be vulnerable with people around you. Some social benefits are:

- Feelings of safety and comfort

- Focus on togetherness
- Increased intimacy
- Increased trust
- Less reliance on social media
- Improved social and familial relationships
- Developing social connections

Stronger Relationships

You can choose to follow the Hygge lifestyle either with friends and family or by yourself. This lifestyle is all about bonding with people and reconnecting. You can also work on nourishing your relationships by spending time with your friends and family. If you stay with your partner, you can have a date night with him or her. Light some candles, put on some beautiful music, change how the living room is organized, cook your favorite meal, and lay out a blanket in the living room. You and your partner can cuddle under the blanket. You can also invite your friends and family over for a movie night. If there is some movie that you have not watched, make it a Hygge night. Create a Hygge atmosphere by turning the lights down, using candles, adding more cushions and pillows to the couch, making some tea and hot chocolate, vegetable sticks with hummus, and popcorn. Make these nights the best moments in your life.

Slows Your Thumb

This does sound funny, doesn't it? The worst thing to do when you lead the Hygge lifestyle is to scroll through your smartphone mindlessly. You can scroll mindlessly through your phone at times, but this is not an activity that will allow you to rest. When you follow the Hygge lifestyle, you need to ensure that you set some time aside to rest. Swap your phone for a book. People can be entertained easily, but when you follow this lifestyle, you need to be keen on relaxation. Leave your phone in the other room and commit yourself to the moment. Yes, your thumb will get a little break.

Remember that Hygge is not just a trend, but a state of mind. You will learn to live in the moment and treasure each moment. If you do not understand this, think about the following situations – playing fetch with your dog or walking in the park. Hygge welcomes and invites togetherness. When you turn your phone off and focus on your life, you will be keener to spend time with the people around you.

Chapter Three: Using Hygge in Your Life

People enjoy feeling cozy, happy, and peaceful, and you do not have to move to Denmark if you want to embrace this lifestyle. You can incorporate different elements of Hygge in your living space and life. When you implement these elements in your lifestyle, you can bring out feelings of connection, comfort, and peace in your life.

Lighting

It is important to improve your lighting if you want to add some elements of Hygge to your living space. The use of soft and warm white light will create a comfortable and inviting space when compared to harsh and bright white bulbs. The bulb will be brighter if the bulb has more lumens. You can install a dimmer if you want to monitor the lighting in the space where you are living. One of the other things to do is to have floor lamps instead of overhead lighting. The latter will create light that will be too bright for the room. It can make the room seem a little institutional. When you use table and floor lamps, you can create a room that is intimate with the best lighting. You should also ensure that you light those areas where people relax, talk to each other, or read. Candles are the best part of following a hyggelig lifestyle. These candles create a soft and warm light that will leave you with a sense of comfort and relaxation. If an open-flamed candle creates a hazard for your living room because of children or pets, you can use LED lights.

Lighting is a crucial element in creating a hygge atmosphere, influencing mood, and contributing to an overall sense of comfort. This chapter explores the significance of lighting in the context of hygge.

Emphasize the preference for warm, soft lighting over harsh or bright lights. Delve into how the right lighting can create a cozy and inviting ambiance. Discuss the role of candles in hygge. Explore the ritual of lighting candles, the comfort they bring, and the soft glow that enhances the hygge experience. Explore alternative lighting options, such as string lights, table lamps, or floor lamps. Provide guidance on choosing fixtures that emit a warm and inviting glow. Acknowledge the importance of natural light. Encourage the arrangement of spaces to maximize exposure to daylight, fostering a connection with the natural elements. Share ideas on how to create hygge-specific nooks with carefully selected lighting, such as a reading corner or a space for quiet contemplation. Recommend the use of dimmer switches to control the intensity of light, allowing for flexibility in creating different moods throughout the day. Discuss the significance of evening rituals involving dimmed lights, such as winding down before bedtime or creating a tranquil atmosphere for relaxation. Extend the discussion to outdoor spaces, emphasizing the importance of soft outdoor lighting for evening gatherings or moments of reflection. Stress the need for a balanced lighting scheme that complements the overall decor and contributes to a harmonious hygge environment. Include some simple DIY lighting projects that readers can undertake to add a personal touch to their spaces. This could involve crafting homemade lanterns or creating unique lighting fixtures.

Texture

Hygge is about using things that feel cozy and soft. You should incorporate accessories like pillows, blankets, rugs, and throws if you want to create a space that is inviting and warm.

These soft textures will calm you down, especially when your anxiety runs very high. Soft textures will also allow you to give people some sense of safety. The way you decorate the living space will allow people to open up with each other. Any conversation you have with other people will feel more open and calmer in this space. Nobody will feel pressured or rushed.

Texture plays a significant role in enhancing the tactile and sensory aspects of a hygge environment. This chapter delves into the importance of incorporating varied textures to create a cozy and comforting atmosphere.

Discuss the preference for soft, tactile materials such as wool, cotton, and faux fur in furniture, throws, and cushions. Highlight the comfort these materials bring to living spaces. Emphasize the concept of layering textures to add depth and visual interest.

Explore how combining different materials contributes to a multi-sensory hygge experience. Introduce the idea of incorporating natural textures like wood and stone.

Discuss how these elements can create a connection with nature and contribute to a grounded, earthy ambiance.

Explore the role of rugs and carpets in defining spaces and adding a soft underfoot feel. Discuss how these elements contribute to the overall warmth of a room.

Encourage the use of handmade items, such as knitted blankets or crocheted pillow covers, to add a personal touch and celebrate craftsmanship.

Discuss innovative ways to introduce texture to walls, such as textured wallpaper or woven wall hangings.

Explore how these elements can transform the character of a room. Highlight the importance of comfortable bedding with varied textures.

Discuss the pleasure of sinking into soft sheets and the warmth provided by layered blankets. Emphasize the sensory appeal of texture in creating a space that invites touch, promoting a sense of well-being and relaxation. Extend the discussion to outdoor environments, exploring how textures like outdoor rugs, cushions, and natural materials contribute to a hygge garden or patio. Include some simple DIY projects that focus on adding texture, such as creating hand-knitted cushions or repurposing materials to craft unique textured decor.

Décor

You can create a calming environment by using different accessories like indoor plants, wood elements, and clean and simple décor. You should use these pieces, especially those that have a special meaning. You can keep pictures of friends, family, and loved ones on the mantel in your living room. You can also place some albums on the coffee table with some pictures of your experiences and travels that you may have shared with the people around you. Hygge is about connection and warmth, so you should use the décor to draw your friends and family in, and create conversation.

The décor in a hygge-inspired space plays a crucial role in creating a cozy and personalized atmosphere. This chapter explores how to approach décor with a focus on simplicity, warmth, and personal touches.

Emphasize the principle of simplicity in hygge décor. Discuss how minimalist design elements contribute to a clean and uncluttered space. Encourage readers to incorporate personal items with sentimental value into their décor.

Discuss how these touches can create a sense of connection and tell a story. Explore the use of nature-inspired elements in décor, such as botanical prints, wooden accents, or natural motifs.

Discuss how these elements bring a touch of the outdoors inside. Highlight the significance of candles in hygge décor. Discuss various types of candles and creative ways to display them using different candle holders. Discuss the role of cozy throws and blankets as both functional and decorative items. Explore how these additions contribute to the overall warmth and comfort of a space. Discuss the idea of creating a gallery wall or displaying photographs that evoke positive memories. Explore how these personal touches contribute to a sense of well-being. Encourage the selection of artwork that holds personal meaning. Discuss how art with emotional significance can enhance the overall atmosphere of a room. Explore a hygge-inspired color palette, emphasizing neutral tones, warm whites, and muted hues. Discuss how these colors contribute to a calm and harmonious environment. Discuss the idea of changing décor with the seasons. Explore how incorporating seasonal elements can keep the space fresh and dynamic throughout the year. Encourage readers to consider repurposing or upcycling existing items for décor. Discuss how these sustainable practices align with the mindful principles of hygge. Include simple DIY projects that readers can undertake to create personalized décor items. This could include crafting homemade candles, creating a gallery wall, or making hand-painted ceramics.

Warmth

You must understand that warmth is not only about the temperature in the room, but also a sense of emotional warmth.
One of the best ways to lead a hyggelig lifestyle is to construct a fireplace.

However, this is not an option for everybody. You can do anything that will create a warm, inviting space, and this will be a plus. Some examples are using candles, displays, accent lighting, and more. You can also use twinkly or fairy lights in some areas of your house if you want to create warmth. These alternate forms can be used as replacements for fireplaces.

The concept of warmth in hygge goes beyond just temperature; it encompasses a sense of emotional and physical comfort. This chapter explores how to infuse warmth into your surroundings to create a hygge-inspired environment. Revisit the role of soft textiles and furnishings in creating warmth.

Discuss how items like plush cushions, soft blankets, and comfortable seating contribute to a cozy atmosphere. Explore furniture choices that evoke warmth, such as wooden pieces or those with soft, inviting textures. Discuss the impact of furniture on the overall feel of a space.

Discuss the traditional significance of fireplaces in hygge. Explore how the warmth of a crackling fire contributes to both the physical and emotional aspects of hygge. Reiterate the importance of warm lighting, exploring different light sources that create a soft and inviting glow. Discuss the impact of lighting on the perceived warmth of a space. Revisit the use of warm colors in décor. Explore earthy tones, muted reds, and warm neutrals, discussing how these hues contribute to a sense of coziness. Discuss how the concept of warmth can be adapted to different seasons. Explore ideas for creating warmth in winter through blankets and candles, and in summer through light and airy textures.

Highlight the warmth that comes from personal connections and social interactions. Discuss the importance of cultivating meaningful relationships within the context of hygge. Encourage the extension of warmth to personal attire. Discuss the joy of wrapping oneself in comfortable, cozy clothing, whether it's a warm sweater or soft socks.

Discuss the idea of creating warm, intimate nooks within a space. Explore how these designated areas contribute to a sense of security and comfort. Explore the role of warm beverages and comfort food in enhancing the hygge experience. Discuss the ritual of enjoying a hot drink or a comforting meal in creating a sense of well-being. Discuss the mindfulness of warmth, encouraging readers to be present and appreciative of the comfort that warmth brings to their lives.

Color

The colors you choose for the living room can help you set a cozy stage for yourself, friends, and family. It is best to choose some neutral colors like soft whites, whites, soft browns, and blushes. When you use neutral colors, you can calm your mind and create a calm atmosphere. These colors will fit into this style of living. The Hygge lifestyle is about creating a soft, comfortable, soothing, or calm atmosphere. In simple words, the Hygge lifestyle will promote an environment that is anti-anxiety for spending time with those you love.

Color plays a crucial role in setting the mood and atmosphere of a hygge-inspired space. This chapter explores the use of color in creating a harmonious, calm, and inviting environment.

Emphasize the use of neutral colors as a foundation for a hygge-inspired palette. Discuss the calming effects of whites, creams, and muted tones in creating a serene backdrop. Explore the incorporation of warm earth tones, such as soft browns, warm grays, and muted greens. Discuss how these hues contribute to a grounded and natural feel.

Discuss the use of soft pastels, such as gentle blues and blush pinks, in creating a delicate and soothing ambiance. Explore how pastels can add a touch of warmth without being overpowering. Emphasize the importance of muted and subdued color choices. Discuss how these tones contribute to a sense of tranquility and understated elegance.

Explore the concept of using carefully chosen accent colors to add pops of interest.

Discuss the impact of small, intentional bursts of color in creating focal points within a space.

Discuss drawing inspiration from nature in choosing color schemes. Explore the calming influence of colors found in natural elements, such as warm wood tones and soothing blues. Encourage readers to select colors that resonate with them personally.

Discuss how individual color preferences can contribute to a sense of connection and well-being. Discuss adapting color choices with the seasons. Explore how transitioning color palettes with the changing seasons can bring a dynamic and ever-evolving aspect to a space. Explore how coordinating color choices with various textures enhances the overall hygge experience. Discuss the interplay between color and texture in creating a cohesive design. Emphasize the mindfulness of color choices, encouraging readers to be intentional and aware of the emotions different colors evoke. Discuss how this mindfulness contributes to a harmonious environment.

Discuss how color can be a form of personal expression. Encourage readers to experiment with color in a way that reflects their unique style and personality.

People

As mentioned earlier, the Hygge lifestyle focuses only on building and maintaining meaningful connections with your loved ones. The objective is always to be present. When you nurture such relationships, you will allow yourself and the people around you to experience a sense of calm. When you are in an environment that you belong, you will feel emotionally secure. When you can maintain emotional safety, you can create a positive social experience. This will allow you to feel the benefit of calm, connection, and ease.

In the context of hygge, the presence and connection with others play a vital role in creating a warm and welcoming atmosphere. This chapter explores the social aspect of hygge, emphasizing the importance of relationships and shared experiences. Emphasize the value of spending quality time with loved ones.

Discuss the joy that comes from shared experiences and meaningful interactions. Explore the idea of intimate gatherings with close friends and family.

Discuss the coziness that comes from smaller, more personal gatherings. Discuss the importance of building strong connections with others.

Explore how fostering deep, meaningful relationships contributes to a sense of belonging and well-being. Highlight the significance of shared meals in hygge.

Discuss the joy of preparing and enjoying food together, creating a sense of unity and connection. Encourage readers to focus on creating a welcoming atmosphere for guests.

Discuss the impact of hospitality in fostering a sense of hygge during social gatherings.

Discuss the idea of unplugging during social interactions. Explore how being present and engaged without the distraction of technology enhances the quality of time spent together.

Explore the joy of celebrating milestones and achievements with others.

Discuss how acknowledging and commemorating special moments strengthens relationships. Emphasize the importance of cultivating positive relationships in various aspects of life. Discuss how supportive and uplifting connections contribute to a sense of hygge. Encourage an inclusive approach to social connections. Discuss how embracing diversity and different perspectives enriches the hygge experience. Discuss the role of mindful communication in nurturing relationships. Explore the importance of active listening and open, honest dialogue. Explore the idea of creating rituals or traditions with others. Discuss how shared rituals contribute to a sense of continuity and shared history. Acknowledge the importance of balancing social interactions with moments of solitude. Discuss how both aspects contribute to a well-rounded and fulfilling lifestyle.

By focusing on the social aspect of hygge, this chapter aims to guide readers in fostering meaningful connections, creating warm and inviting social spaces, and celebrating the joy that comes from shared experiences. If there are specific social dynamics or nuances you'd like to explore further, feel free to provide additional guidance.

Activity

A hyggelig lifestyle will involve things that will help you feel cozy, connected, and peaceful. You will learn to connect with the people around you with ease.

One of the best ways to do this is to spend time with friends and family. These gatherings are focused only on connections with the people around you and not only on the environment. You do not have to make it a black-tie affair.

The Hygge lifestyle will only suggest the opposite. These gatherings will offer you to create a space that is inviting, casual, and also offers people space where they can focus on connecting with the people around them.

This environment will allow them to feel comfortable. You can organize a game night with friends, family, or neighbors, host a book night, or invite people over for coffee or dinner.

The concept of hygge extends beyond physical spaces and décor—it also encompasses activities that contribute to a sense of joy, relaxation, and connection.

This chapter explores various hygge-inspired activities that readers can integrate into their daily lives. Encourage the joy of cozy reading.

Discuss the pleasure of immersing oneself in a good book while surrounded by soft blankets and a warm ambiance. Explore the idea of engaging in comfortable and enjoyable hobbies.

Discuss how activities like knitting, drawing, or playing a musical instrument can contribute to a hygge lifestyle. Discuss the therapeutic benefits of mindful crafting.

Explore activities such as DIY projects, creating handmade gifts, or engaging in creative pursuits that bring a sense of accomplishment. Encourage readers to connect with nature through leisurely walks. Discuss the calming effect of spending time outdoors and appreciating the beauty of the natural world. Highlight the joy of cooking together with loved ones.

Discuss the collaborative and rewarding aspects of preparing and sharing meals as a group. Explore the nostalgic joy of playing board games or solving puzzles.

Discuss how these activities promote friendly competition, teamwork, and shared moments of laughter. Discuss the role of music and singing in creating a hygge atmosphere.

Explore the joy of playing musical instruments, listening to favorite songs, or even singing along with others. Encourage the creation of special hygge evenings.

Discuss the idea of dedicating specific times to hygge activities, such as cozy movie nights, storytelling, or stargazing.

Discuss the importance of taking breaks from technology. Explore activities that allow individuals to unplug, such as digital detox days, and embrace simple, analog pastimes. Explore the joy of celebrating seasons and holidays in a hygge manner. Discuss traditions, rituals, and activities that bring a sense of warmth and festivity to different times of the year. Discuss the benefits of mindful meditation. Explore simple meditation practices that promote relaxation, mindfulness, and a sense of inner peace. Encourage the practice of journaling. Discuss how writing down thoughts, gratitude, and reflections can be a therapeutic and mindful activity.

By exploring a variety of hygge-inspired activities, this chapter aims to inspire readers to infuse their lives with moments of joy, relaxation, and connection. If there are specific activities or themes you'd like to focus on, or if you have any preferences regarding the depth of exploration, feel free to provide additional guidance.

Some Tips

Here are a few tips you can use to follow a hyggelig lifestyle.
Light Candles
Wiking says that you cannot follow a Hygge lifestyle if you do not have any candles. This is mentioned in the first chapter of the book. When you turn the lights down and light candles around your house, you can transform the atmosphere you are in with ease. To make this better, you can use scented candles that will bring tranquility to space. It is impossible for you not to enjoy the relaxing effects of the aroma or the glow of the flame. The smell and aroma are a big part of the Hygge lifestyle. If some scents or fragrances remind you of something wonderful when you felt comfortable and safe, it will smell like Hygge.
Never Deprive Yourself

You must ensure that you enjoy the little pleasures in your life. It also means that you need to indulge in whatever you feel like and that you are kind to yourself. The Danes are crazy about treats and other confectionaries like licorice and gummy bears. You must ensure that you do not focus only on eating healthy and always take the opportunity to indulge in those delights that you well-deserve.

Drink a Hot Cup of Tea

Have you always felt better after you sipped a hot cup of tea while you were wrapped in a cozy, warm blanket? If you did, then you should relish a cup of peppermint tea or any other flavored tea that you like. Wiking has an emergency Hygge list that ties into the joy of taking a break and the Hygge philosophy of comfort.

Unwind

Hygge does encourage you to spend time with the people you love. However, this does not mean that you should always have people around you. One of the best things about the Hygge lifestyle is that you should take a moment and pamper yourself. You can apply a facemask, repair your skin with the best moisturizing formula, or anything else that will help you unwind. You can also slather on some lotion, take a bath, or even paint your nails. You must appreciate this form of downtime if you want to follow the Hygge lifestyle.

Create a Playlist

The right tunes will always set the right mood. When you create a playlist that will complement your evening with your friends and family or evening by yourself, you can invite more positive vibes and coziness into the room. You can also destress your body easily. Install speakers and play the music you love.

Bring the Outdoors Inside

Danes hate sitting indoors during winter, so they love bringing the outdoors inside the house.

They love everything that is made out of wood, including natural items like nuts, twigs, plants, and more. The smell of the fireplace and other wooden objects will make you feel closer to nature. These items are simple and stick to the concept of Hygge. You can find the right objects that will embody the outdoors with musk and other textured woods.

Keep a Book Handy

You also need to keep a book handy. This is an extremely important thing to do. After a long, hard day, it is better to get lost in the pages of a book. This book could be a biography, how-to-guide, or favorite novel. Make sure you pick a book that will put you at ease. Do not skim through the book since this will not be a very hyggelig thing to do. Let the story unfold and see where it goes. You should take everything in.

Unplug

For most people, their devices are their lifelines. When you put your phone down and turn off the computer, even if it is for an hour, you are doing yourself a favor. This may seem like a very difficult thing to do, but it will help you learn to be more present. You will learn to be more present in your space. This is an important thing about Hygge. Hygge will help you tell your mind when you are off duty.

Make Your Space Cozy

Big blankets and pillows are extremely necessary. This is especially true if you want to evoke a sense of warmth and create a comfortable environment. You can always make the environment cozier by adding more pillows and blankets. You can use calming ingredients like patchouli, chamomile, and lavender to improve the space. These fragrances will bring in a sense of security and peacefulness. It is essential to create a safe environment if you want to make your house more hyggelig.

Add Twinkly Lights

It is ideal to have twinkly lights at home. As mentioned earlier, the lighting is the best part of a Hygge lifestyle. These lights are festive and cheery, and they look great anywhere. You can use these lights in your living room, bedroom, or even on the patio.

Light a Fire

One of the best parts about the Danish culture is to huddle around the fire. This fire can either be indoors or outdoors. This is the perfect time for you to spend time with your friends, family, and loved ones. You should always be thankful for the company you keep. A fireplace will represent togetherness and warmth. This is the place where people will enjoy spending time with their loved ones.

Open Presents at the Right Time

This is a concept that you will find in many Hygge books. This is an extremely important concept to remember. It is always a good idea to open some special packages when you want to celebrate your goals or milestones. When you learn to appreciate these purchases, you will learn to link every item in your house with some happy memories.

Planning Hygge Factors in Every Room

When you redo your house, you will plan the décor in your room. When you did this, you probably did not pay too much attention to the emotional aspect of the décor. You also did not think about all the memories you would be creating in these rooms. Hygge will allow you to plan the elements in every room. For example, if you were worried about the wallpaper in your room when you were redoing the house, you would not have thought about how it would affect your morning routines or reading at night. You will soon learn to decorate your house so that you can make yourself and the people you love feel more at home.

Chapter Four: Embracing Hygge at Work

One of the best places to practice Hygge is at work. Let us look at some examples of how you can do this at work.

Bring a Mug to Work

As mentioned earlier, you must sip warm beverages frequently if you want to follow the Hygge lifestyle. Caffeine is one of the best ways to boost your energy. It will also help you focus on your work. It is always a good idea to grab a cup of coffee with your colleagues. Make sure that you talk about anything other than work. Bring a coffee mug from home and use that at work. When you drink out of your favorite mug, you will be carrying a piece of home to work. You should never be afraid to take a refill or give your brain a little break from some mundane tasks.

Encouraging the simple act of bringing a mug to work is a delightful way to infuse hygge into the workplace. This subchapter can explore the various dimensions of this small yet impactful ritual.

Discuss how bringing a personal mug to work can immediately transform a generic workspace into a more personalized and inviting environment.

Explore the psychological comfort that comes from using a familiar mug.

Discuss how the routine of having a favorite mug can create a sense of stability and well-being. Encourage readers to choose a mug that resonates with them. Whether it's a favorite color, a humorous message, or a nostalgic design, the chosen mug should evoke positive feelings.

Highlight the ritualistic aspect of making tea or coffee in the workplace.

Discuss how taking a few minutes to prepare a hot beverage can be a mindful and comforting break. Encourage the idea of creating a small hygge corner in the workspace.

Discuss how adding elements like a cozy blanket or a small plant can enhance the overall hygge ambiance. Discuss the social aspect of bringing a mug to work. Encourage interactions with colleagues, whether it's sharing a tea break or starting a conversation about each other's mugs. Emphasize the importance of taking mindful breaks during the workday. Discuss how sipping a warm beverage from a cherished mug can be a simple yet effective way to reset and recharge. Explore the idea of incorporating hygge-inspired drinks. Discuss the joy of experimenting with different teas, coffees, or hot chocolates to find the perfect comforting beverage. Encourage readers to personalize their mugs further. Discuss the possibility of decorating or customizing mugs as a creative and enjoyable activity. Discuss the idea of building a collection of meaningful mugs over time. Whether it's collecting mugs from different places or receiving them as gifts, each mug can tell a story. Explore how bringing a mug from home to work is a symbolic way of bringing elements of comfort and home into the professional environment.

Create a Playlist

As mentioned earlier, you should try to create a playlist. Remember, music does a lot for the mind. You should make a playlist of calming upbeat tunes. You can include some acoustic songs that will help you get through your day. Wiking says in his book that you should create a playlist with slow songs.

Curating a hygge-inspired playlist is a wonderful way to infuse warmth and joy into daily life. This subchapter can guide readers on how to create a music collection that complements the cozy ambiance of their spaces.

Encourage the selection of music genres known for their calming and comforting qualities. Explore options such as acoustic, folk, classical, or ambient music.

Discuss the importance of personalization. Encourage readers to include songs and artists that resonate with their individual preferences and evoke positive emotions. Highlight the soothing effect of instrumental music and soft vocals. Discuss how these elements can contribute to a serene and tranquil atmosphere. Encourage the creation of a diverse playlist. Discuss the benefits of including a variety of songs, from instrumental pieces to lyrical tracks, to cater to different moods and occasions. Discuss how the playlist can be curated for various activities. For example, a calming instrumental playlist might be suitable for reading, while a more upbeat selection could be ideal for cooking or socializing. Explore the idea of incorporating seasonal or weather-inspired tunes. Discuss how music can enhance the connection with the changing seasons and create a harmonious atmosphere. Discuss the social aspect of music. Encourage the creation of collaborative playlists with friends or colleagues, fostering a sense of shared musical experiences. Highlight the importance of mindful listening. Discuss how actively engaging with the music, rather than using it as background noise, can amplify the positive effects. Encourage readers to include their favorite comfort tracks. Discuss the emotional connection that certain songs may have and how they can serve as a source of solace. Explore the addition of nature sounds or ambient recordings to the playlist. Discuss how these elements can bring an extra layer of tranquility to the listening experience. Discuss the importance of regularly updating and refreshing the playlist. Encourage readers to add new discoveries and remove songs that may have become overly familiar. Explore the idea of tailoring playlists for specific spaces. Discuss how the music in a living room playlist might differ from a playlist intended for a home office or bedroom.

Take Time to Unwind

When you take a break for lunch, you should ensure that you take a break. You should not plan your assignments, stare at the computer while you eat, or even check your email. Make sure that you take a complete break. If the climate outside is nice, you should take a walk. You can take a walk in the park or even walk around the block, depending on where you work. Regardless of what it is that you do, you should make sure to go outdoors. This will help you unwind and explore the area around your workplace to lift your spirits.

Encouraging readers to take intentional breaks and unwind is a fundamental aspect of embracing hygge in daily life. This subchapter explores various ways individuals can prioritize relaxation and rejuvenation.

Discuss the importance of scheduling dedicated breaks throughout the day. Encourage readers to step away from work or responsibilities to take short moments for themselves. Explore the idea of creating a personal relaxation ritual. Discuss how establishing a routine or set of activities before bedtime or after work can signal the transition to a more relaxed state. Introduce simple mindful breathing exercises. Discuss the benefits of deep, intentional breaths in reducing stress and promoting a sense of calm.

Highlight the significance of disconnecting from digital devices. Discuss the impact of taking a break from screens to reduce mental clutter and promote a more peaceful mindset. Encourage the joy of reading for pleasure.

Discuss the therapeutic benefits of immersing oneself in a captivating book as a means of escapism and relaxation. Explore the practice of gentle stretching or yoga. Discuss how incorporating these activities can release physical tension and promote a sense of well-being.

Discuss the rejuvenating effects of spending time in nature. Encourage readers to take short walks outside, listen to birdsong, or simply enjoy the natural surroundings to unwind. Reiterate the hygge ritual of enjoying a warm beverage. Discuss how the act of brewing and savoring a cup of tea or coffee can be a mindful and comforting break. Discuss the benefits of mindful napping. Encourage readers to embrace short, intentional naps to recharge energy levels and enhance overall well-being. Introduce the practice of journaling for reflection. Discuss how jotting down thoughts, feelings, or gratitude can be a therapeutic way to unwind and gain perspective. Highlight the role of calming music in the unwinding process. Discuss how creating a playlist of soothing tunes can be a quick and effective way to shift into a more relaxed state. Discuss the value of embracing unplanned moments of stillness. Encourage readers to pause, take a few deep breaths, and appreciate the present moment as a way to unwind throughout the day.

Decorate Your Workspace

You should always decorate the workplace with some items from home. You can have some pictures of your family or even some flowers on your desk. If you want to follow a Hygge lifestyle, you can also bring some string lights that you can drape around your desk. Make sure always to have plenty of tea on hand and some vintage books that you can read during your break. Stick to your company's policies, but decorate your desk. You should never think of your office as a mundane or practical space. You should make it a special or comfortable haven where you are productive and inspired. If the company allows you to use candles, you can light a small one at your desk for ambiance and glow. You should make the environment feel more like home using artwork, sentimental items from home, or a cozy chair.

Transforming a mundane workspace into a hygge-inspired haven can greatly enhance one's daily experience. This subchapter explores creative and practical ways to decorate a workspace for comfort and productivity.

Encourage the use of personalized desk accessories. Discuss how items like a favorite mug, a unique pen holder, or a small plant can add a touch of personality to the workspace.

Discuss the importance of warm lighting in a workspace. Encourage the use of desk lamps with soft, warm bulbs or the addition of string lights to create a cozy ambiance. Explore the incorporation of soft textiles.

Discuss the idea of adding cushions or a cozy throw to the chair, creating a more comfortable and inviting seating area. Encourage the use of inspiring wall art.

Discuss how displaying motivational quotes, personal photographs, or artwork can contribute to a positive and uplifting atmosphere.

Discuss the introduction of natural elements. Encourage the use of small potted plants, succulents, or even a vase of fresh flowers to bring a touch of nature into the workspace.

Highlight the importance of decluttering for focus. Discuss how a clean and organized workspace promotes a sense of calm and makes the environment more conducive to productivity.

Discuss the significance of comfortable seating. Encourage readers to invest in an ergonomic chair or to add a cushion for extra comfort during long working hours.

Explore the use of aromatherapy in the workspace. Discuss the benefits of using essential oil diffusers or scented candles to create a pleasant and calming atmosphere. Discuss the benefits of desk plants and greenery.

Encourage the use of low-maintenance plants that not only add visual appeal but also contribute to a healthier indoor environment.

Discuss the idea of creating a flexible work arrangement. Encourage readers to consider alternative seating options or standing desks to change their working positions throughout the day. Explore the creation of an inspiration board or vision board. Discuss how visualizing goals and aspirations can serve as a motivational and uplifting element in the workspace. Encourage the use of a coordinated color scheme. Discuss how selecting a harmonious color palette for desk accessories, wall decor, and textiles can create a visually pleasing and cohesive look. Discuss the use of personalized scent diffusers. Encourage readers to choose scents that they find calming or invigorating to enhance the sensory experience of their workspace.

Host a Potluck

The Hygge lifestyle is the source of everything hygge, and the best way to have a workspace that is hyggelig is to savor a home-cooked meal with your colleagues at work. You can taste each other's cooking as well.
Organizing a potluck is a wonderful way to embrace hygge by fostering a sense of community and sharing. This subchapter explores the steps to host a potluck gathering that is both enjoyable and stress-free.
Discuss the initial steps of planning, including sending out invitations and coordinating contributions. Emphasize the collaborative nature of potlucks and how everyone can play a part. Encourage the idea of having a theme or coordinating the cuisine.
Discuss how a themed potluck adds an extra layer of fun and creativity, and how coordinating ensures a balanced and diverse meal. Highlight the importance of creating a cozy atmosphere. Discuss how arranging seating, adding soft lighting, and incorporating comfortable elements contribute to a welcoming environment.

Discuss the joy of comfort foods at potlucks. Encourage participants to bring dishes that evoke feelings of warmth and nostalgia, contributing to a hygge-inspired culinary experience. Emphasize the sharing of recipes and stories behind the dishes.

Discuss how this exchange creates a sense of connection and adds a personal touch to the culinary experience. Discuss the idea of setting up a beverage station. Encourage the inclusion of warm beverages like tea, coffee, or mulled cider to complement the meal and enhance the hygge atmosphere. Suggest creating a collaborative playlist for the potluck.

Discuss how a carefully curated playlist adds to the ambiance and encourages a shared musical experience. Highlight the importance of comfortable seating arrangements. Discuss how arranging chairs and adding cushions or throws creates a relaxed and inviting space for guests. Encourage the practice of mindful eating.

Discuss how taking the time to savor each bite and engage in conversation enhances the overall enjoyment of the meal. Discuss the importance of expressing gratitude.

Encourage hosts and guests to express appreciation for the shared meal, the effort put into each dish, and the joy of coming together. Emphasize the simplicity of potluck gatherings.

Discuss how the collaborative effort minimizes the stress on the host, allowing everyone to focus on the enjoyment of the event. Suggest the idea of creating a memory corner. Encourage guests to bring a small memento or share a brief story, creating a space for collective memories and connections. Discuss the thoughtfulness of providing takeaway containers. Encourage guests to take home leftovers, extending the enjoyment of the potluck beyond the event.

Do Good

Regardless of whether you bring a box of donuts or chocolates to work or simply compliment your colleagues, you can turn their entire day around. All you need to do is be kind. When you support someone, you can help them manage stress. When you have someone to care for you, you will become more resilient. When you are vulnerable to people, you can distribute the stress that you carry.

Embracing the spirit of kindness and generosity is a core aspect of hygge. This subchapter explores various ways in which individuals can incorporate acts of goodwill into their lives, fostering a sense of connection and community.

Encourage readers to engage in random acts of kindness. Discuss how small gestures, such as holding the door for someone or leaving a thoughtful note, can have a significant positive impact.

Highlight the benefits of volunteering. Discuss how contributing time and skills to local community organizations or charitable causes can create a sense of purpose and fulfillment.

Discuss the importance of supporting local businesses. Encourage readers to choose local shops and artisans, fostering a sense of community and contributing to the well-being of the neighborhood. Explore the concept of sharing resources.

Discuss how individuals can contribute to community initiatives, such as food drives or clothing donations, to support those in need. Encourage acts of generosity among friends. Discuss how sharing skills, offering assistance, or simply being present for others can strengthen bonds and create a supportive community.

Highlight the connection between hygge and environmental stewardship. Encourage eco-friendly practices, such as reducing waste, recycling, and adopting sustainable habits that contribute to the well-being of the planet. Discuss the role of gratitude in doing good. Encourage readers to cultivate a culture of gratitude by expressing appreciation for others, acknowledging kindness, and fostering positive relationships. Encourage participation in local community events.

Discuss how attending or organizing events, such as neighborhood clean-ups, festivals, or cultural gatherings, strengthens community bonds. Discuss the significance of donating to charities. Encourage readers to contribute to causes they believe in, whether through financial donations, in-kind contributions, or fundraising efforts. Encourage the support of friends' creative or entrepreneurial ventures. Discuss how championing the efforts of friends and acquaintances contributes to a culture of encouragement and shared success. Discuss the impact of kindness in the workplace. Encourage colleagues to engage in acts of kindness, such as offering assistance, expressing appreciation, or creating a positive and collaborative work environment. Highlight the value of teaching and mentoring. Encourage individuals to share their knowledge and skills with others, fostering a culture of learning and growth within the community. Emphasize the importance of celebrating diversity and inclusion. Discuss how embracing differences and promoting an inclusive environment contributes to the well-being of the community.

Embrace Teamwork

Team spirit is an integral part of the Hygge lifestyle. Right from their childhood, Danes work together in groups. They are always taught to either give or seek advice or help in terrible situations.

They are told to stay confident regardless of their weaknesses and stay humble. Danish families work as a team. You can organize some team activities that will encourage all of you to work together. You can use different activities like scavenger hunts or tournaments.

When people are aware of hygge, they will be more aware of the special and small moments in their lives.

The spirit of collaboration and teamwork aligns seamlessly with the principles of hygge. This subchapter explores how individuals can foster a sense of togetherness, support, and shared success within a team or group setting.

Discuss the importance of building a supportive and collaborative culture within a team. Encourage open communication, active listening, and a sense of camaraderie. Emphasize the significance of recognizing and appreciating team members. Discuss how expressing gratitude and acknowledging each other's contributions fosters a positive and motivating work environment.

Discuss the benefits of collaborative decision-making. Encourage teams to involve members in discussions and decision processes, fostering a sense of shared ownership and responsibility. Highlight the value of team-building activities. Discuss how engaging in collaborative exercises or outings can strengthen interpersonal relationships and build a sense of unity.

Discuss the importance of creating and aligning with a shared vision. Encourage teams to collaboratively define goals, values, and aspirations, fostering a sense of purpose and direction.

Emphasize the inclusion of diverse perspectives. Discuss how embracing different viewpoints and backgrounds within the team leads to richer ideas and more innovative solutions.

Discuss the role of teamwork in supporting individual growth. Encourage mentorship and collaborative learning opportunities within the team to help members develop their skills and expertise.

Highlight the necessity of clear communication channels. Discuss how effective communication ensures that team members are well-informed, reducing misunderstandings and fostering trust. Discuss the joy of celebrating team milestones. Encourage the acknowledgment of achievements, both big and small, as a way to boost morale and reinforce a sense of accomplishment. Emphasize the importance of flexibility and adaptability within a team. Discuss how a willingness to adjust plans and strategies collaboratively contributes to overall resilience. Discuss the role of empathy and understanding in teamwork. Encourage team members to be supportive of each other's challenges and triumphs, creating a compassionate work environment. Highlight the value of encouraging and providing constructive feedback. Discuss how open feedback loops contribute to continuous improvement and the overall success of the team. Emphasize the concept of shared responsibility. Discuss how a sense of collective accountability within the team fosters a supportive and collaborative work culture. Discuss the importance of nurturing team bonds. Encourage social interactions, team lunches, or activities outside of work that contribute to a strong sense of camaraderie.

Chapter Five: How to Make Your Garden Hygge

We have looked at how to make your home Hygge, so let us look at how to make your back yard Hygge. It is easier to Hygge your garden than your house since you have a lot of room to experiment with. The views, experiences, and scents from your garden are some things you will enjoy.

Bonfires

Most people do not have fireplaces inside the house, so it is fun if you have an open fire in the garden. This is easier to handle, as well. All you need is a fire bowl or fire pit. Add some charcoal and logs to the bowl or pit and light the fire. You can have some other supplies like biscuits, chocolates, sticks, and marshmallows. If you want to have the perfect moment, you can invite your friends and family over.

Incorporating bonfires into your life can bring a sense of warmth, connection, and coziness, perfectly aligning with the principles of hygge. This subchapter explores the various aspects of enjoying bonfires in different settings.

Encourage the idea of hosting outdoor gatherings with bonfires. Discuss how the crackling flames create a focal point for socializing and how the warmth invites people to gather around.

Discuss the importance of selecting a suitable location for the bonfire. Consider safety, local regulations, and the availability of seating to ensure a comfortable and enjoyable experience. Emphasize the importance of fire safety.

Discuss basic fire safety precautions, such as keeping a safe distance, having a fire extinguisher nearby, and ensuring the fire is fully extinguished afterward. Explore cozy seating arrangements around the bonfire. Discuss the use of comfortable outdoor furniture, blankets, and cushions to enhance the hygge atmosphere.

Highlight the joy of preparing and sharing comfort foods like s'mores around the bonfire. Discuss how simple treats contribute to a sense of indulgence and shared enjoyment. Encourage stargazing and storytelling during bonfires. Discuss how the flickering flames create a captivating backdrop for sharing stories, creating lasting memories, and fostering a sense of connection.

Discuss the versatility of bonfires for both intimate evenings and larger gatherings. Encourage readers to adapt the size of the bonfire to fit the occasion and create the desired ambiance. Explore the idea of hosting seasonal bonfire celebrations. Discuss how different times of the year, such as summer solstice or autumn evenings, provide unique opportunities to enjoy bonfires.

Highlight the addition of live music or acoustic performances. Discuss how the warmth of a bonfire enhances the acoustic experience, creating a cozy and intimate setting for musical enjoyment. Discuss the charm of bonfires at the beach. Encourage readers to experience the unique ambiance of beach bonfires, combining the sound of waves with the crackling of the fire.

Encourage the creation of a hygge nook around the bonfire. Discuss how thoughtful lighting, soft blankets, and comfortable seating contribute to a cozy and inviting space. Emphasize the practice of mindful presence during bonfires. Discuss the simple pleasure of being fully present, enjoying the warmth, and savoring the moment with friends and loved ones.

Discuss how the warmth and coziness experienced around a bonfire can inspire the transition to indoor hygge settings. Encourage readers to carry the spirit of the bonfire into their homes.

Embracing the View

You cannot always spend a lot of time in your garden, especially during extreme climates. So, make sure to design your garden, keeping the view in mind. You can look at the view as a picture in a frame. Look at the garden from every room inside your house and see what aspects you can change. You can then add some color to the garden and make the view work. Whenever you look at the garden, it will be a little more special.

Taking time to appreciate and connect with your surroundings is an integral part of hygge. This subchapter explores the practice of embracing the view, whether it's from your home, a favorite spot, or during outdoor activities.

Encourage the creation of cozy spaces that highlight a beautiful view. Discuss how arranging furniture, adding soft textiles, and optimizing lighting can enhance the overall experience.

Highlight the concept of viewing windows as frames for the outside world. Discuss how framing a beautiful view with well-designed windows can bring nature into the indoor space.

Encourage the creation of outdoor seating areas. Discuss how comfortable chairs, cushions, and blankets can transform a backyard or balcony into a cozy spot for enjoying the view. Discuss the joy of incorporating morning rituals with a view.

Encourage readers to start their day by sipping coffee or tea while taking in the surroundings, fostering a sense of calm and gratitude. Explore the beauty of seasonal changes. Discuss how embracing the different colors of each season—spring blossoms, summer greens, autumn foliage, or winter snow—adds variety and appreciation to the view. Emphasize the practice of mindful observation.

Discuss how taking a few moments each day to simply observe the view, appreciating the details and changes, contributes to a sense of mindfulness. Discuss the importance of optimizing indoor lighting to enhance the view. Encourage the use of soft and warm lighting that complements the natural beauty outside.

Explore ways to connect with nature through the view. Discuss activities like birdwatching, identifying plants, or simply listening to the sounds of the outdoors as ways to deepen the connection.

Encourage the creation of a reading nook with a view. Discuss how positioning a comfortable chair or window seat near a picturesque view can create an ideal spot for relaxation and reading. Discuss the pleasure of outdoor meals with a view. Encourage readers to set up meals or gatherings in locations that offer a scenic backdrop, enhancing the overall dining experience.

Highlight the tranquility of evening reflections. Discuss the calming effect of watching the sunset or city lights in the evening and how it can serve as a reflective and serene time. Encourage the artistic appreciation of the landscape.

Discuss how viewing the outdoors as a living canvas can inspire creativity and a deeper connection to the natural world. Discuss the idea of creating visual points of interest in the view. Encourage the addition of features like garden art, fountains, or well-placed lighting to enhance the visual appeal.

Little Things Count

You must focus on every single detail, including the big views. You can have a small table in the garden where you have a plant in a terracotta pot with pansies and violas on the table. You can install some fountains or place some sculptures between the plants. Make sure that you make an effort to make your garden look pretty. It will take you some time to set up the perfect garden, but once you have it, you can look at it every day.

Appreciating the small details in everyday life is a fundamental aspect of hygge. This subchapter explores the significance of finding joy and comfort in the little things that contribute to a sense of well-being and coziness.

Encourage the practice of mindful morning rituals. Discuss how simple acts like sipping a favorite beverage, enjoying a warm shower, or taking a moment to stretch can set a positive tone for the day.

Highlight the importance of sensory pleasures. Discuss the joy of engaging the senses, whether through the aroma of freshly brewed coffee, the warmth of a soft blanket, or the texture of a favorite book.

Discuss the impact of personalizing living spaces. Encourage readers to surround themselves with items that hold sentimental value or bring a sense of comfort, creating a personalized and hygge-infused environment. Emphasize the beauty of quiet moments.

Discuss the joy of taking short breaks to appreciate the stillness, listen to calming sounds, or engage in moments of solitude as a way to recharge. Encourage gratitude practices. Discuss the positive effects of reflecting on and expressing gratitude for the small, positive aspects of life, fostering a mindset of appreciation.

Discuss the pleasure of savoring meals. Encourage readers to take time to enjoy each bite, appreciate the flavors, and create a mindful dining experience, whether alone or with loved ones. Explore the simplicity of nature walks.

Discuss how taking a short stroll in a nearby park, garden, or natural setting allows individuals to connect with the outdoors and find joy in the little wonders of nature.

Highlight the cozy ambiance created by candlelight and soft lighting. Discuss how the gentle glow of candles or soft lighting contributes to a warm and comforting atmosphere, especially during evenings. Encourage the art of handwritten notes and letters. Discuss the personal touch and emotional connection that comes from sending or receiving handwritten messages, fostering a sense of intimacy. Discuss the simple pleasures found in food and drink. Encourage readers to savor a favorite snack, indulge in a comforting beverage, or experiment with small culinary delights that bring joy. Emphasize the act of capturing everyday moments. Discuss the value of documenting life's simple joys through photography, journaling, or other creative means to create a visual record of happiness. Explore the comfort provided by cozy textiles. Discuss the joy of wrapping oneself in a soft blanket, lounging in comfortable pajamas, or enjoying the tactile pleasure of quality fabrics. Highlight the importance of expressing affection. Discuss how small gestures of love, such as a hug, a smile, or a kind word, contribute to a positive and uplifting atmosphere. Encourage the escape found in reading. Discuss how getting lost in a good book, whether fiction or non-fiction, provides a mental retreat and an opportunity for relaxation.

Introduce Scented Flowers

You must fill your garden with some scents. It is easy to introduce these fragrances by planting the right flowers in the garden.

You can plant honeysuckle if you want to have some beautiful smells in winter. You can also have some fences in your garden and plant creepers or climbers that have beautiful fragrances.

Enriching your surroundings with the delightful fragrance of scented flowers is a sensory experience that perfectly aligns with the principles of hygge. This subchapter explores the beauty and benefits of incorporating scented flowers into your living spaces.

Encourage the selection of fragrant flower varieties. Discuss popular choices such as roses, jasmine, lavender, lilacs, or lilies, highlighting their unique scents and potential positive effects on mood.

Discuss the art of creating indoor flower arrangements. Encourage readers to place scented flowers in vases or containers strategically positioned in living rooms, bedrooms, or other frequently used spaces.

Highlight the dual purpose of scented flowers as natural air fresheners. Discuss how the gentle fragrance can replace artificial scents, creating a fresh and inviting atmosphere within the home. Encourage the placement of scented flowers in relaxation spaces.

Discuss how having fragrant blooms in areas where individuals unwind, such as reading nooks or meditation corners, enhances the overall sense of tranquility. Discuss the role of scented flowers in creating a bedroom oasis. Encourage readers to place flowers on bedside tables or dressers, bringing a touch of nature and a soothing aroma to the space. Explore the idea of creating seasonal flower displays.

Discuss how different seasons offer a variety of scented blooms, allowing individuals to rotate and enjoy the changing fragrances throughout the year. Encourage the creation of DIY scented potpourri. Discuss how dried petals from scented flowers can be used to make potpourri, providing a long-lasting and visually appealing way to enjoy their fragrance.

Highlight the aromatherapy benefits of scented flowers. Discuss how the natural aromas can contribute to stress relief, relaxation, and improved mood, aligning with the holistic well-being promoted by hygge. Discuss the synergy of pairing scented flowers with candles. Encourage the use of scented candles that complement the floral fragrances, creating a harmonious and cozy ambiance. Emphasize the practice of mindful flower appreciation. Discuss the importance of taking a moment to intentionally notice and enjoy the scent of the flowers, promoting a mindful connection with nature. Encourage the cultivation of scented flower gardens. Discuss how individuals can plant fragrant flowers in their outdoor spaces, creating a private oasis where they can enjoy the natural scents. Discuss the sensory delight of combining textures and scents. Encourage the arrangement of scented flowers alongside soft textiles, creating a multi-sensory experience that appeals to both touch and smell. Explore the use of floral essential oils. Discuss how infusing living spaces with the aroma of floral essential oils extracted from scented flowers can provide a continuous and customizable fragrance.

Do Not Forget the Lights

You cannot forget about the lights. Yes, it is true, you cannot have many candles in your garden, but you can have some white fairy lights. These lights will allow you to recreate the magic of candles. You can string them over the fence or hang them on a wall.

Lighting plays a crucial role in creating a cozy and inviting atmosphere, making it an essential element of the hygge lifestyle. This subchapter explores the significance of different lighting techniques and fixtures to enhance the warmth and ambiance of living spaces.

Encourage the use of warm and soft lighting. Discuss how the choice of bulbs with warm color temperatures creates a cozy and comforting ambiance, reminiscent of the gentle glow of candlelight.

Highlight the charm of string lights and fairy lights. Discuss how these delicate lights, whether hung indoors or outdoors, add a touch of magic and create a whimsical atmosphere in the home.

Emphasize the timeless appeal of candles and candle holders. Discuss the role of candles in providing not only soft illumination but also a sense of ritual and tranquility, aligning with the hygge philosophy.

Discuss the use of lanterns and hurricane lamps. Encourage readers to incorporate these classic lighting fixtures, as they not only provide practical illumination but also contribute to the overall coziness of a space.

Highlight the warmth and visual appeal of a fireplace or fire pit. Discuss how the flickering flames create a focal point, contributing to a hygge-inspired ambiance, especially during colder seasons.

Discuss the benefits of adjustable and dimmable lighting. Encourage the use of fixtures that allow individuals to control the intensity of light, adapting to different activities and moods throughout the day. Explore the use of paper lanterns and shades.

Discuss how these soft and diffused lighting options add an elegant touch to the decor while creating a gentle and inviting glow. Discuss the unique charm of Himalayan salt lamps. Encourage readers to consider these natural ionizers that emit a soft, warm glow, promoting a serene and calming atmosphere.

Highlight the cozy appeal of table lamps with fabric shades. Discuss how the diffusion of light through fabric creates a soft and inviting glow, contributing to the overall hygge ambiance. Emphasize the safety and versatility of LED candles and fairy lights.

Discuss how these battery-operated alternatives provide a risk-free way to enjoy the ambiance of candles and string lights. Discuss the use of overhead pendant lights. Encourage the selection of fixtures that complement the overall decor while providing focused and ambient lighting in key areas of the home. Encourage the creation of personalized lighting nooks. Discuss how strategically placing lamps or fixtures in cozy corners, reading nooks, or relaxation spaces enhances the intimate and comforting atmosphere. Explore the harmony of combining natural and artificial light. Discuss how balancing daylight with carefully chosen artificial lighting creates a harmonious and well-lit environment.

Enjoy Outdoors In a Better Way

You can spend some time in the garden once you have it set up. You can watch the sunrise, sunset or stars on clear nights. If you want to take it one step further, you can install a sauna or hot tub in your garden. You can also go camping in your backyard if you want to.

Enhancing your outdoor experiences contributes to a more fulfilling and hygge-inspired lifestyle. This subchapter explores ways to make the most of outdoor spaces, fostering a connection with nature and creating inviting environments.

Encourage the use of comfortable outdoor seating. Discuss the importance of investing in quality outdoor furniture, cushions, and throws to create a cozy and inviting space for relaxation. Highlight the use of weather-resistant textiles. Discuss the benefits of choosing outdoor textiles that can withstand various weather conditions while maintaining a soft and comfortable feel.

Discuss the concept of outdoor living rooms. Encourage readers to set up designated areas with seating, rugs, and lighting, creating an extension of their indoor living space in the open air.

Explore the charm of portable fire pits. Discuss how these versatile additions provide both warmth and a focal point for outdoor gatherings, fostering a sense of togetherness and relaxation.

Emphasize the use of cozy blankets and throws. Discuss how having warm textiles readily available for cooler evenings encourages individuals to spend more time outdoors, even as the temperature drops.

Encourage outdoor dining experiences. Discuss the joy of al fresco meals, whether it's a simple breakfast on the patio or a leisurely dinner under the stars, enhancing the overall enjoyment of meals.

Highlight the eco-friendly appeal of solar-powered outdoor lighting. Discuss the use of solar lanterns, string lights, or path lights to illuminate outdoor spaces in the evenings, creating a magical ambiance.

Discuss the importance of gardens and greenery. Encourage the cultivation of plants, flowers, and green spaces, creating a visually appealing and refreshing outdoor environment.

Explore the delight of bird feeders and baths. Discuss how attracting birds to the outdoor space adds a natural element, providing entertainment and a sense of connection with the surrounding ecosystem.

Encourage the creation of outdoor reading nooks. Discuss how arranging comfortable seating, shade, and lighting in a designated outdoor reading spot allows individuals to enjoy books amidst nature.

Discuss the soothing effect of water features. Encourage the addition of fountains, ponds, or even a small water feature to create a tranquil ambiance and enhance the overall outdoor experience. Emphasize the concept of creating a relaxation zone. Discuss how thoughtful placement of hammocks, lounge chairs, or recliners can transform outdoor spaces into havens for relaxation and unwinding.

Highlight the enjoyment of outdoor music. Discuss the use of outdoor-friendly music systems or portable speakers, allowing individuals to create a soundtrack for their outdoor activities and gatherings. Encourage stargazing and sky appreciation. Discuss the simple pleasure of looking up at the night sky, whether it's identifying constellations, watching meteor showers, or enjoying the moonlight. Discuss practical insect-repellent solutions. Encourage the use of natural repellents, candles, or plants to create a comfortable outdoor environment without the nuisance of insects.

Build a Fort

You may have constructed a fort in your backyard as a child and would have played there every single day. You can have just as much fun even now in a fort. You can work with your kids and build a den. Make this den cozy and spend time there every day. Share some food in the den and have a little picnic. You can tell your kids stories about how you enjoyed the den as a child.

The whimsical and creative act of building a fort is a delightful way to infuse a sense of playfulness and coziness into your living space. This subchapter explores the joy of fort-building, a cherished activity that aligns with the principles of hygge.

Encourage readers to choose a cozy corner for fort-building. Discuss how selecting a space with soft lighting and enough room for cushions and blankets sets the stage for a comfortable and inviting fort.

Discuss the fun of gathering materials. Encourage readers to collect blankets, pillows, cushions, and any other soft and cozy items that can contribute to the construction of their fort. Provide step-by-step guidance on blanket fort construction.

Discuss different techniques for draping blankets over furniture, creating walls with cushions, and ensuring a stable and secure structure.

Highlight the charm of adding fairy lights or string lights. Discuss how the soft glow of lights can transform the fort into a magical space, creating a warm and cozy atmosphere.

Emphasize the importance of soft textiles. Discuss the joy of layering blankets and cushions inside the fort, creating a plush and comfortable space for relaxation and play. Discuss the delight of including snacks and drinks. Encourage readers to bring their favorite treats into the fort, whether it's a cup of hot cocoa, snacks, or a selection of comfort foods. Explore the versatility of the fort as a reading nook or movie corner.

Discuss how adding a pile of books, magazines, or a tablet for watching movies enhances the fort experience. Encourage the incorporation of games. Discuss how individuals or families can enjoy board games, card games, or even create their own fort-specific games to enhance the sense of playfulness. Highlight the inclusion of music.

Discuss the joy of creating a playlist of favorite tunes or calming melodies to accompany the fort-building experience, enhancing the overall ambiance. Discuss the fort as a cozy retreat. Encourage readers to view the fort as a personal sanctuary—a space to unwind, relax, and escape the outside world, aligning with the hygge philosophy. Explore the option of sharing the fort experience.

Discuss how building a fort can become a shared activity with family or friends, fostering a sense of togetherness and creating lasting memories. Emphasize that fort-building is for all ages. Discuss how both children and adults can enjoy the creative process and the comfort of spending time in a well-crafted fort. Encourage the documentation of fort creations. Discuss the idea of taking pictures or creating a journal to capture the different forts built over time, creating a visual record of cherished moments.

Let the Games Begin

If you organize game nights with friends and family, make sure to have it outdoors. You can play games like a treasure hunt, Risk and other games. If you want, you can play Twister in your yard, too. Just place the Twister sheet on a blanket.

Incorporating games into your hygge-inspired lifestyle adds an element of joy, connection, and shared experiences. This subchapter explores various games and activities that align with the principles of hygge, fostering a sense of togetherness and enjoyment.

Encourage the use of board games for cozy evenings. Discuss popular board games that are well-suited for small groups or families, creating an atmosphere of friendly competition and laughter.

Highlight the charm of card games for intimate gatherings. Discuss classic card games or introduce new ones that are easy to learn, allowing individuals to engage in spirited play while enjoying each other's company.

Discuss the mindfulness of puzzle nights. Encourage the assembly of jigsaw puzzles, crossword puzzles, or other challenging yet relaxing activities that promote focused engagement and tranquility. Explore outdoor games for fresh air fun.

Discuss activities like bocce ball, cornhole, or frisbee that can be enjoyed in outdoor spaces, combining the pleasure of gaming with the benefits of nature. Acknowledge video games for cozy solo time. Discuss how video games, especially those with immersive and calming elements, can provide individuals with a form of relaxation and entertainment in their personal space. Encourage DIY game nights with friends.

Discuss the idea of creating custom games or adapting existing ones to suit the preferences and personalities of the group, fostering a unique and memorable experience. Highlight the excitement of trivia and quiz nights.

Discuss how organizing themed trivia sessions or quizzes can be a fun way to challenge knowledge, spark interesting conversations, and create a sense of camaraderie. Discuss role-playing games for unleashing creativity. Encourage the exploration of tabletop role-playing games that allow participants to immerse themselves in imaginative and collaborative storytelling.

Explore the nostalgia of retro games. Discuss the joy of revisiting classic video games, board games, or card games from the past, creating a sense of nostalgia and shared memories. Acknowledge app games for casual enjoyment. Discuss mobile games that are easy to pick up and play, making them suitable for short bursts of entertainment or as a way to unwind during downtime. Encourage game nights within book clubs. Discuss how incorporating games into book club meetings can add an extra layer of enjoyment, providing a balance between literary discussions and lighthearted play. Highlight seasonal game tournaments. Discuss the idea of organizing game tournaments during specific seasons, creating a sense of anticipation and friendly competition among participants. Discuss mindful gaming for relaxation. Encourage the selection of games that promote relaxation, stress relief, and mindfulness, allowing individuals to unwind and recharge through gaming experiences. Emphasize the creation of family game traditions. Discuss how regularly engaging in games can become a cherished family tradition, fostering bonds, communication, and a sense of unity.

Bring the Outside Inside

The Danish love is for incorporating some natural elements into their homes, and they love doing this in winter. You should do this to make your house a little more Hygge. You can go for a walk and find some pinecones or flowers and place them in your home. You can add the pinecones to a bowl in your living room and the flowers to a vase. Greenery can breathe life into any space, and you can do this to make your house feel more like home.

Integrating elements of nature into your indoor spaces is a key aspect of hygge, promoting a sense of harmony and connection with the outdoors. This subchapter explores creative ways to bring the outside inside, enhancing the overall coziness of your living environment.

Encourage the use of indoor plants and greenery.

Discuss popular houseplants that not only add aesthetic appeal but also contribute to improved air quality, creating a fresh and natural atmosphere. Highlight the use of natural materials in decor. Discuss the incorporation of materials like wood, stone, or woven fibers in furniture, accessories, and decor items, creating a tactile connection to nature.

Discuss the charm of nature-inspired artwork. Encourage the display of paintings, prints, or photographs featuring landscapes, botanicals, or wildlife, bringing the beauty of nature into the indoor space. Emphasize the importance of open windows. Discuss how allowing fresh air to circulate through open windows creates a connection with the outdoors, invigorating the indoor environment.

Explore ways to enhance natural light. Discuss techniques such as using sheer curtains, mirrors, or light-colored decor to maximize the entry of natural light, creating a bright and uplifting indoor atmosphere. Encourage the arrangement of seating with outdoor views.

Discuss how positioning seating areas near windows or glass doors allows individuals to enjoy the beauty of the surrounding landscape from the comfort of their homes.

Discuss the use of outdoor-inspired color palettes. Encourage the selection of earthy tones, greens, blues, or other colors reminiscent of nature to create a calming and harmonious color scheme. Highlight scented candles with nature scents. Discuss the use of candles infused with fragrances like pine, eucalyptus, or citrus to bring the invigorating scents of the outdoors into indoor spaces. Discuss seasonal decor transitions. Encourage individuals to update decor elements with the changing seasons, bringing in seasonal flowers, foliage, or themed decor to reflect the beauty of nature throughout the year. Emphasize the use of natural fiber textiles. Discuss the incorporation of materials like cotton, linen, or wool in blankets, throws, and cushions, adding a touch of nature's comfort to indoor spaces. Discuss rock or shell collections as decor. Encourage the display of collected rocks, shells, or other natural treasures, creating a personal and visually appealing connection to outdoor environments. Explore the tranquility of water features. Discuss the placement of indoor fountains or water features that mimic the sound of flowing water, bringing a sense of calmness and the outdoors into the home. Encourage nature-inspired sounds. Discuss the use of soundscapes or recordings of nature sounds, such as birdsong, ocean waves, or rustling leaves, to create a soothing auditory connection to the outdoors. Highlight botanical prints and patterns. Discuss the incorporation of floral or botanical patterns in decor items, upholstery, or linens, adding a touch of nature's beauty to indoor spaces.

Chapter Six: Some Tips to Follow Hygge

You now have an idea of what Hygge is and the changes you must make to lead a Hygge life. This chapter will shed some light on the tips you can follow to make the transition easier.

Stick to Neutral Color Schemes

Remember always to use neutral colors at home. The colors you use at home should not overwhelm you, especially if you want to lead a Hygge lifestyle. Regardless of what objects or items you wish to add to your home, you must ensure that they only contribute toward developing an atmosphere of peace and harmony. When you want to create a relaxing space, you need to stick to neutral color schemes. Use pastel colors like browns, creams, and light grays if you want to create a comfortable area, where you and your friends or family to enjoy.

Choosing neutral color schemes is a fundamental principle of hygge design, creating a calm and soothing backdrop that promotes comfort and a sense of harmony.

This subchapter explores the benefits and strategies of sticking to neutral color palettes in various aspects of home decor. Discuss the fundamental appeal of neutrals.

Encourage readers to appreciate the versatility and timeless elegance that neutral colors bring to interior spaces, setting the stage for a hygge-inspired environment. Emphasize the use of neutral wall colors.

Discuss the calming effect of neutral tones such as whites, beiges, grays, or soft pastels on walls, creating a blank canvas that allows other elements to shine. Highlight the versatility of neutral furniture.

Discuss how choosing sofas, chairs, and tables in neutral tones provides a sense of cohesion, allowing for easy integration of different decor elements over time. Encourage the layering of neutral textiles. Discuss the use of blankets, throws, cushions, and rugs in neutral shades to add warmth, texture, and a sense of coziness to living spaces.

Discuss the charm of natural wood finishes. Encourage the use of wooden furniture or decor items with natural wood tones, adding warmth and a touch of nature to the neutral color scheme.

Emphasize the tranquility of neutral bedding. Discuss the benefits of using neutral-colored bedding and linens, creating a serene and inviting atmosphere in bedrooms for restful sleep. Highlight the role of accessories in neutral tones. Discuss how decor items such as vases, candles, and artwork in neutral colors contribute to a cohesive and visually pleasing overall aesthetic.

Discuss the elegance of monochromatic color schemes. Encourage readers to explore the beauty of sticking to a single neutral color in varying shades, creating a sophisticated and harmonious look. Emphasize neutrals in kitchen and dining areas. Discuss the use of neutral tones for cabinetry, countertops, and dining sets, creating a timeless and inviting atmosphere for cooking and dining.

Discuss the tranquility of neutral bathrooms. Encourage the use of neutral tiles, fixtures, and linens in bathrooms, fostering a spa-like retreat that promotes relaxation and self-care. Highlight the extension of neutrals to outdoor spaces.

Discuss how neutral-toned outdoor furniture, cushions, and decor items create a seamless transition between indoor and outdoor living areas. Discuss the importance of textures in a neutral palette.

Encourage the use of varied textures, such as woven fabrics, knits, and natural materials, to add depth and visual interest to neutral spaces. Emphasize the adaptability and timelessness of neutral design. Discuss how a neutral color scheme provides a versatile foundation, allowing individuals to easily update decor elements or introduce seasonal accents. Discuss the opportunity for personalization. Encourage readers to infuse their personality into neutral spaces through artwork, personal collections, or unique decor items, creating a home that reflects their individual style.

Creating a Comfortable Atmosphere

You now know that coziness is the objective when you choose to switch to a Hygge lifestyle. One of the easiest ways to do this is to fill your house with fluffy pillows and comforters. Snuggle up on your couch or bed with layers of pillows and blankets. Create an environment where you can unwind. You can create a love seat or window bench. You can relax in these areas, either with a cup of hot coffee or a good book. This will ensure you can get enough peace.

Establishing a comfortable atmosphere is at the heart of the hygge lifestyle. This subchapter delves into the essential elements and practices that contribute to a cozy and inviting ambiance within your home.

Emphasize the importance of soft and inviting seating. Discuss the choice of comfortable sofas, chairs, and cushions that beckon individuals to relax and unwind, fostering a sense of coziness.

Encourage the use of plush textiles and throws. Discuss the addition of soft blankets and throws on sofas and chairs, providing both physical warmth and a visual invitation to snuggle up. Highlight the role of cushions for comfort.

Discuss the arrangement of cushions in various shapes and sizes to enhance seating comfort and create a welcoming and plush environment.

Discuss the warmth brought by layered rugs. Encourage the use of rugs in different textures and sizes to add a soft underfoot feel and visually define specific areas within a room. Emphasize the importance of warm lighting. Discuss the use of soft, warm-toned lighting sources such as lamps, candles, and string lights to create a gentle and inviting glow in living spaces. Discuss the cozy ambiance of a fireplace or candlelight. Encourage the use of fireplaces, candles, or flameless alternatives to introduce a warm and flickering element that enhances the overall atmosphere. Encourage the incorporation of personalized decor. Discuss the importance of surrounding oneself with meaningful items, photographs, or mementos that evoke positive emotions and contribute to a cozy atmosphere. Explore the benefits of aromatherapy. Discuss the use of scented candles, essential oil diffusers, or incense to infuse delightful and calming scents into the living space, enhancing the overall sensory experience. Emphasize the value of uncluttered spaces. Discuss the concept of maintaining a clutter-free environment to create a serene atmosphere that promotes relaxation and a sense of order. Discuss the incorporation of nature-inspired elements. Encourage the use of natural materials, plants, or artwork featuring natural motifs to bring a touch of the outdoors inside, fostering a connection with nature. Highlight the use of soft color palettes. Discuss the calming effect of pastel or muted color schemes that contribute to a tranquil and comfortable visual environment. Discuss the arrangement of furniture for coziness. Encourage adaptable layouts that facilitate conversation, create intimate seating arrangements, and optimize the flow of movement within a room. Emphasize the importance of comfortable bedding. Discuss the use of soft and cozy sheets, blankets, and pillows to create a welcoming and snug sleeping environment in bedrooms. Discuss the role of background music or sounds. Encourage the use of calming music, nature sounds, or white noise to provide a soothing auditory backdrop that complements the comfortable atmosphere. Explore the charm of hygge-inspired reading nooks. Discuss the creation of cozy reading corners with comfortable seating, good lighting, and soft textiles, inviting individuals to immerse themselves in a book. Emphasize the practice of hygge rituals. Discuss the importance of establishing comforting routines, whether it's enjoying a cup of tea, reading a book by candlelight, or simply taking moments of quiet reflection.

Adding Some Texture

You may not think about texture when you think about cozy Hygge décor. When you introduce some texture in your living space, you can add some interesting attributes to a minimalist design. Incorporate natural and warm materials like wool and wood to your décor. If you want to add a pop of color, you can add different flowers to the décor.

Introducing texture is a key element in creating a visually interesting and tactilely inviting space, aligning with the principles of hygge design. This subchapter explores the art of incorporating different textures to enhance the coziness and warmth of your living environment.

Encourage the use of layered textiles. Discuss the arrangement of various soft materials such as cushions, throws, and blankets to create a tactile and inviting atmosphere in seating areas.

Highlight the importance of plush upholstery. Discuss the choice of sofas and chairs with soft, touchable fabrics, providing both comfort and visual appeal in the living space.

Discuss the charm of rich and cozy knits. Encourage the use of knitted blankets, cushions, or even upholstery to add a warm and textural element that invites touch and evokes a sense of comfort. Emphasize the use of natural fiber rugs.

Discuss the benefits of incorporating rugs made from materials like jute, sisal, or wool, adding a layer of texture to the floor and creating a cozy feel. Explore the functionality of woven baskets. Discuss how woven baskets not only serve as practical storage solutions but also contribute a tactile and rustic texture to the decor. Discuss the warmth brought by wooden elements. Encourage the inclusion of wooden furniture, decor items, or even accent walls to introduce a natural and comforting texture to the living space. Highlight the use of textured wall coverings. Discuss options such as textured wallpaper, reclaimed wood panels, or textured paint finishes that add depth and interest to the walls. Discuss the luxurious comfort of faux fur. Encourage the use of faux fur throws, cushions, or even rugs to bring a touch of opulence and coziness to seating areas. Emphasize the importance of tactile bedding. Discuss the use of bedding with different textures, such as linen, cotton, or jersey, to create a sumptuous and inviting bed for restful sleep. Discuss the comfort of cushioned headboards. Encourage the choice of beds with padded or upholstered headboards, adding a soft and inviting texture to the bedroom. Highlight the elegance of velvet upholstery. Discuss how velvet-covered furniture, such as sofas or chairs, can add a touch of luxury and sophistication while providing a lush and tactile experience. Encourage the juxtaposition of textures. Discuss the visual interest created by combining smooth textures, like glass or metal, with rough textures, such as natural fibers or distressed wood, for a balanced and eclectic look. Discuss the role of tactile decorative objects. Encourage the inclusion of decor items with interesting textures, such as ceramic vases, woven sculptures, or stone figurines, to enhance visual and tactile appeal. Explore layered window treatments. Discuss the combination of curtains, blinds, or shades with different textures to not only control light but also add depth and coziness to the room. Highlight the beauty of embroidered or textured fabrics. Discuss the use of fabrics with intricate patterns, embroidery, or textured weaves in upholstery, curtains, or cushions to create a sense of craftsmanship and detail. Emphasize textured tableware. Discuss the use of dishes, placemats, or tablecloths with textured surfaces, adding a tactile element to dining experiences and enhancing the overall sensory pleasure.

Redo Your Bathroom

Make your bathroom a place where you can relax. Do not use it only to take a quick shower every morning. After a long day at work, you can enter the bathroom and relax and rejuvenate. Ensure that you create a bathroom that is both peaceful and pleasant. Remove unwanted clutter in the bathroom, like the laundry and other items. To do this, you can ensure that you have hidden storage space. You can also invest in scented candles, essential oils, diffusers, and comfortable robes.

Transforming your bathroom into a cozy and inviting space aligns with the hygge lifestyle, promoting a sense of relaxation and self-care. This subchapter explores practical and aesthetic considerations for redoing your bathroom with a hygge-inspired touch.

Emphasize the use of soft and absorbent towels. Discuss the importance of investing in high-quality towels in neutral or calming colors to enhance the sensory experience after bathing. Highlight the luxury of heated towel racks.

Discuss the installation of heated towel racks to add an extra layer of warmth and comfort, especially during colder seasons. Encourage the use of cozy bath mats. Discuss the selection of plush and soft bath mats or rugs to provide a warm and comfortable surface for bare feet. Discuss the incorporation of natural elements.

Encourage the use of materials like wood, stone, or bamboo in bathroom decor items, creating a connection to nature and adding warmth to the space. Highlight the importance of soft lighting. Discuss the use of gentle and warm lighting fixtures to create a relaxing ambiance in the bathroom, enhancing the overall comfort.

Discuss the choice of a soothing color palette. Encourage the use of calming and neutral colors for bathroom walls, tiles, and accessories to promote a serene atmosphere. Emphasize the benefits of aromatherapy. Discuss the placement of scented candles or essential oil diffusers in the bathroom to infuse soothing scents and create a spa-like experience. Encourage organization and decluttering.

Discuss the importance of well-organized bathroom spaces, using storage solutions to keep toiletries out of sight and create a serene environment.

Discuss the inclusion of plants. Encourage the use of low-maintenance plants, such as ferns or snake plants, to bring a touch of nature into the bathroom and improve air quality. Highlight the addition of comfortable seating.

Discuss the inclusion of a small stool or a comfortable chair, providing a spot for relaxation, reading, or enjoying a moment of tranquility.

Discuss personalized and functional storage. Encourage the use of storage solutions that cater to individual needs, keeping daily essentials within reach while maintaining a clutter-free space. Emphasize the use of luxurious bath products.

Discuss the indulgence of high-quality soaps, bath oils, or bath salts, elevating the bathing experience and contributing to a sense of pampering.

Discuss the placement of mirrors. Encourage the strategic use of mirrors to enhance natural light, create the illusion of space, and add an element of sophistication to the bathroom. Highlight the comfort of soft robes.

Discuss the availability of soft and cozy robes for a post-bath or shower ritual, contributing to the overall feeling of relaxation and comfort. Discuss the inclusion of personalized artwork. Encourage the display of artwork or decor items that resonate with personal preferences, adding a touch of individuality to the bathroom. Emphasize the practice of hygge-inspired rituals. Discuss the importance of incorporating small rituals, such as lighting candles before a bath or playing soft music, to create a sense of comfort and mindfulness.

Use Objects That Tell a Story

Pia Edberg says that some studies show that people who follow Hygge in Denmark shy away from consumerism. If you want to follow a Hygge lifestyle, you should avoid purchasing mass-produced items. Instead, decorate your house with accents and furniture that means something to you. These items could be given to you as gifts, or you may have purchased them when you travel.

Infusing your living space with objects that carry personal meaning and tell a story is a key aspect of creating a hygge-inspired environment. This subchapter explores the significance of incorporating items with personal narratives into your home decor.

Encourage the use of family heirlooms. Discuss the sentimental value and storytelling potential of incorporating heirlooms or antiques into your decor, connecting the present with the past. Highlight the stories behind travel souvenirs.

Discuss the incorporation of mementos from travels, sharing the memories and experiences associated with each item to create a sense of wanderlust.

Emphasize the uniqueness of handcrafted items. Discuss the inclusion of handcrafted or artisanal pieces, each with its own story of craftsmanship and individuality, adding character to your space.

Discuss the storytelling power of photographs. Encourage the display of framed photographs capturing special moments and milestones, turning your walls into a visual narrative of your life's journey.

Encourage the use of books as decor. Discuss the aesthetic appeal of well-loved books or literary treasures, arranged on shelves or coffee tables to showcase personal interests and passions.

Highlight the significance of personal collections. Discuss the integration of items related to hobbies or collections, whether it's stamps, vinyl records, or vintage cameras, expressing your unique interests.

Discuss the importance of meaningful artwork. Encourage the selection of artwork that resonates personally, evoking emotions or memories and serving as a visual expression of your identity.

Emphasize the sentimental value of handwritten items. Discuss the display of handwritten letters, notes, or cards, preserving the personal touch and emotional connection conveyed through the written word. Discuss the sustainability and stories behind repurposed items.

Encourage the use of repurposed or upcycled furniture or decor, each piece with a history and a new chapter in your home. Highlight the generational continuity of items. Discuss the beauty of using items passed down through family generations, connecting different eras and creating a sense of familial continuity.

Encourage the display of personal creations. Discuss the inclusion of your own artwork or creations, whether it's paintings, sculptures, or crafts, adding a touch of your creative spirit to your living space. Discuss the stories behind pieces from significant events.

Encourage the display of items acquired during pivotal life events, such as weddings, graduations, or anniversaries, creating a timeline of cherished memories. Explore the symbolism in decor. Discuss the use of items with symbolic meaning, whether it's religious artifacts, cultural symbols, or tokens that represent personal beliefs and values. Emphasize the value of customization.

Discuss the incorporation of customized or personalized decor items, such as monogrammed linens or engraved keepsakes, adding a personal touch to your surroundings. Encourage the rotation of displayed items. Discuss the idea of periodically refreshing your decor by rotating displayed items, allowing different stories to take center stage and preventing visual monotony.

Be Smart

You should use technology if you want to make your home cozy. You can install some wireless speakers to play the right music to set the mood. It is always a good idea to have a smart home since that will enable you to adjust the lighting, change the temperature, or play the right music through your smartphone. You will no longer have to run from one room to the next to adjust these. This will allow you just to be present.

Incorporating smart and functional elements into your living space aligns with the principles of efficiency and convenience in the hygge lifestyle. This subchapter explores how integrating smart technology and thoughtful design can enhance the comfort and functionality of your home.

Discuss the benefits of smart lighting. Encourage the use of smart bulbs, dimmers, or lighting systems that can be controlled remotely, allowing you to adjust the ambiance according to your preferences and create cozy settings. Emphasize the convenience of home automation.

Discuss the integration of smart home devices, such as thermostats, blinds, or security systems, to enhance comfort and streamline daily routines.

Highlight the utility of voice-activated assistants. Discuss the incorporation of devices like smart speakers or virtual assistants that respond to voice commands, making it easier to control various aspects of your environment.

Discuss the comfort provided by smart thermostats. Encourage the use of thermostats that can be programmed or controlled remotely, ensuring that your home is always at an optimal and cozy temperature. Emphasize the importance of efficient storage.

Discuss the integration of smart storage solutions, such as modular shelving, organizational apps, or custom-built furniture, to maximize space and maintain a clutter-free environment.

Discuss the peace of mind offered by smart security systems. Encourage the use of smart cameras, doorbell cameras, or monitoring systems that provide real-time updates and enhance the security of your home. Highlight the convenience of smart appliances.

Discuss the benefits of incorporating smart kitchen and household appliances, such as refrigerators, ovens, or washing machines, that offer automation and remote control features. Encourage energy-efficient choices. Discuss the use of smart thermostats, LED lighting, or energy monitoring systems to promote sustainability and reduce energy consumption, aligning with the hygge emphasis on mindful living.

Discuss the versatility of smart furniture. Encourage the use of furniture with built-in technology or multi-functionality, such as convertible sofas or smart tables, to optimize space and adapt to various needs. Emphasize the use of digital organizational tools.

Discuss the benefits of apps and digital platforms for task management, scheduling, and organization, helping to streamline daily activities and reduce stress. Highlight the enjoyment of smart entertainment. Discuss the integration of smart TVs, sound systems, or streaming devices that provide easy access to entertainment options, contributing to a cozy and enjoyable home atmosphere. Discuss the importance of smart home office setups. Encourage the use of ergonomic furniture, smart lighting, and technology solutions to create efficient and comfortable workspaces within your home. Emphasize the benefits of smart home maintenance. Discuss the use of apps or devices that monitor home systems, alerting you to potential issues and simplifying the maintenance and upkeep of your living space. Discuss the role of technology in relaxation. Encourage the use of apps, guided meditation programs, or smart devices that promote relaxation and mindfulness, aligning with the hygge emphasis on well-being. Highlight the adaptability of smart home designs. Discuss how smart home features can be integrated into various design styles, ensuring that technology complements the aesthetic and enhances the overall hygge atmosphere.

Be Thankful and Present

Every morning, you should think about what you are most thankful for. Make sure to do this the minute you wake up every morning. It is important to do this. You can also share the one thing about your day that was great with your friends and family. When you do this, you will begin to focus only on the positive aspects of life.

Cultivating a mindset of gratitude and mindfulness is central to the hygge philosophy, promoting a sense of appreciation for the present moment. This subchapter explores practices and perspectives that encourage gratitude and presence within your daily life and living space.

Discuss the benefits of gratitude journaling. Encourage the practice of keeping a journal where you regularly write down things you are thankful for, fostering a positive outlook and mindfulness. Highlight the idea of a gratitude wall. Discuss the concept of dedicating a space in your home to display notes, quotes, or images that represent things you are grateful for, creating a visual reminder of positivity. Discuss the creation of mindful spaces. Encourage the design of a dedicated meditation or mindfulness corner in your home, equipped with comfortable cushions, soft lighting, and perhaps natural elements to promote tranquility. Emphasize the importance of digital detoxing. Discuss the creation of specific zones in your home where digital devices are limited or prohibited, allowing you to disconnect and be present without distractions. Highlight the practice of gratitude during meals. Encourage the tradition of expressing gratitude before meals, whether through a moment of silent reflection, a shared statement, or even a simple acknowledgment of the nourishment received. Discuss the incorporation of daily mindfulness. Encourage small, mindful practices such as savoring a cup of tea, taking a moment of deep breathing, or simply appreciating the sensory details of your surroundings. Emphasize the connection to nature. Discuss the incorporation of natural elements in home decor, such as plants, stones, or wooden accents, to create a grounding environment that encourages presence and gratitude. Encourage family gratitude rituals. Discuss the importance of involving family members in gratitude practices, whether through shared reflections during dinner or creating a collective gratitude jar. Discuss the creation of thankfulness displays. Encourage the arrangement of displays that showcase items or symbols representing gratitude, fostering a visual reminder of the positive aspects of life. Highlight the benefits of outdoor reflection. Encourage gratitude walks or spending time in nature, allowing for reflection on the beauty of the surroundings and fostering a sense of appreciation for the natural world. Discuss the power of daily affirmations. Encourage the practice of incorporating positive affirmations into your daily routine, promoting a mindset of gratitude, self-love, and optimism. Emphasize the use of a gratitude jar. Discuss the concept of maintaining a gratitude jar or box where you regularly deposit notes expressing moments of gratitude, creating a tangible collection of positive memories. Encourage mindful eating practices. Discuss the importance of being fully present during meals, savoring each bite, and appreciating the flavors, textures, and nourishment provided by the food. Highlight the creativity of gratitude projects. Encourage the engagement in art or craft projects that involve expressing gratitude, such as creating a gratitude collage, vision board, or even simple drawings. Discuss the creation of mindful breathing spaces. Encourage the design of areas in your home where you can practice mindful breathing exercises, fostering a sense of calm and presence. Emphasize the idea of gratitude sharing circles. Discuss the practice of gathering with friends or family to share moments of gratitude, creating a supportive and positive atmosphere.

Setting the Table

According to the Hygge philosophy, you must spend enough time with friends and family. You must share a meal with your friends and family, too. You need to have a good dining room table if you are going to do this. The Danes love having wooden tables and handcrafted chairs at home. Make sure to have some earthy designs and set the table with the best food. Creating a welcoming and aesthetically pleasing table setting is a significant aspect of embracing the hygge lifestyle, enhancing the dining experience and fostering a sense of connection. This subchapter explores considerations and practices for setting a hygge-inspired table.

Encourage the use of natural materials. Discuss the benefits of opting for tableware made from materials like wood, ceramic, or stone, adding a touch of nature to the table setting.

Highlight the charm of simplicity. Discuss the appeal of rustic and simple table settings, incorporating minimalistic elements to create an unpretentious and cozy atmosphere.

Discuss the importance of candlelight. Encourage the use of candles, either traditional or flameless, to create a warm and inviting ambiance during meals, contributing to a hygge-inspired atmosphere.

Emphasize the use of soft fabrics. Discuss the incorporation of soft and cozy table linens, such as tablecloths, napkins, or placemats, to add tactile comfort and enhance the overall dining experience. Encourage creativity in tableware selection. Discuss the idea of mixing and matching different sets of tableware, creating an eclectic and personalized look that reflects individual style. Discuss the inclusion of personalized touches.

Encourage the use of place cards, personalized name tags, or small tokens at each place setting, adding a thoughtful and individualized element to the table. Highlight the use of natural decor. Discuss the incorporation of natural elements like flowers, branches, or seasonal greens as centerpieces, bringing a touch of the outdoors to the dining table. Emphasize earthy color choices.

Discuss the appeal of earth-toned color palettes for table settings, using warm and muted hues that evoke a sense of comfort and connection with nature. Discuss the informality of arrangements. Encourage a relaxed approach to table settings, avoiding overly formal arrangements and allowing for a more laid-back and comfortable dining experience. Highlight the uniqueness of handmade items.

Discuss the inclusion of handmade or artisanal tableware, such as pottery or handcrafted ceramics, adding character and individuality to the table setting. Discuss the versatility of seasonal decor.

Encourage transitioning table decor with the seasons, incorporating seasonal elements and colors to create a dynamic and ever-changing atmosphere. Emphasize comfort beyond the table. Discuss the option of placing cozy blankets or throws on dining chairs, allowing guests to wrap themselves in warmth during longer gatherings. Encourage an unfussy approach. Discuss the idea of creating approachable and unfussy table settings, where guests feel comfortable and can focus on the enjoyment of the meal and the company. Highlight the charm of string lights. Discuss the use of string lights to create an intimate and cozy atmosphere, especially for evening or indoor dining occasions. Discuss the concept of hygge-inspired centerpieces. Encourage the use of items like candles, fairy lights, or natural elements as centerpieces, creating a focal point that enhances the hygge ambiance. Emphasize the importance of comfortable seating. Discuss the arrangement of chairs and seating that allows for a relaxed and convivial atmosphere, contributing to the overall comfort of the dining experience. Highlight the benefits of family-style dining. Discuss the practice of serving dishes in the center of the table, encouraging sharing and a communal dining experience.

Take a Walk

You will be in the present when you learn to engage more of your senses. You can take a walk to get closer to nature. You need to absorb the sounds, smells, and sights that come with nature. You should also reward yourself with a slice of cake or hot drink after the walk.

Incorporating the simple yet profound act of taking a walk aligns with the hygge emphasis on connecting with nature, promoting mindfulness, and embracing a slower pace of life. This subchapter explores the benefits and considerations of incorporating walks into your routine.

Discuss the benefits of nature walks. Encourage taking walks in natural settings, such as parks or wooded areas, to promote mindfulness, reduce stress, and foster a connection with the environment. Highlight the charm of urban strolls. Discuss the enjoyment of exploring neighborhoods, urban parks, or local streetscapes on foot, discovering hidden gems and fostering a sense of community. Emphasize the value of solo walks. Discuss the benefits of taking walks alone, providing time for self-reflection, mental clarity, and the opportunity to appreciate the surroundings at one's own pace. Encourage walking with others. Discuss the social aspect of walking with friends, family, or pets, fostering connection, meaningful conversations, and shared moments of enjoyment. Highlight the beauty of seasonal walks.

Discuss the idea of adapting walks to different seasons, appreciating the changing landscapes, colors, and atmospheres that each season brings. Discuss the practice of walking meditation.

Encourage the integration of mindfulness into walks by paying attention to each step, the rhythm of breathing, and the sensory experiences of the surroundings.

Emphasize the concept of hygge-inspired walking rituals. Discuss the idea of incorporating rituals into walks, such as carrying a warm drink, listening to calming music, or simply enjoying the sensory aspects of the environment. Highlight the importance of unplugging during walks. Discuss the benefits of taking a break from digital devices during walks, allowing for a more immersive and present experience with the surroundings. Discuss walking as a mode of commuting.

Encourage the consideration of walking for short commutes when feasible, providing an opportunity to integrate physical activity into daily routines. Encourage photography during walks. Discuss the idea of bringing a camera or using a smartphone to capture interesting sights during walks, fostering creativity and a deeper appreciation for the environment. Highlight the importance of varied routes.

Discuss the benefits of exploring different walking trails, routes, or neighborhoods to keep the experience fresh and engaging. Emphasize the importance of comfortable footwear. Discuss the necessity of wearing comfortable shoes for walks, ensuring an enjoyable experience and preventing discomfort. Discuss the value of an unhurried pace. Encourage a slow and leisurely pace during walks, allowing time to observe, appreciate, and savor the surroundings without feeling rushed. Highlight the practice of mindful breathing.

Discuss incorporating conscious breathing into walks, promoting relaxation and mindfulness as you synchronize breath with each step. Encourage scheduled walk breaks. Discuss the idea of incorporating short walks into the daily schedule, providing moments of rejuvenation and contributing to overall well-being. Discuss dressing comfortably for walks. Encourage the use of cozy and weather-appropriate clothing, embracing a hygge-inspired wardrobe that enhances comfort during outdoor strolls. Emphasize observation and gratitude. Discuss the practice of observing the details of the environment during walks and expressing gratitude for the ability to experience the beauty around you.

Be Here Now

You must ensure that you are glued to the present. Never worry about what is happening on the Internet. You do not have to get rid of electronic items if you want to switch to the Hygge lifestyle. All you need to do is put them aside and be with the people around you. Make sure that you put your phones away when you meet your friends and family.

Embracing the present moment and cultivating mindfulness are core principles of the hygge lifestyle. This subchapter explores the concept of "Be Here Now" as a guiding philosophy, encouraging individuals to fully engage with and appreciate the current moment.

Discuss the practice of mindful breathing. Encourage simple breathing exercises that help individuals center themselves, alleviate stress, and foster a sense of presence. Highlight grounding techniques. Discuss methods, such as focusing on the senses or connecting with the physical environment, to anchor oneself in the present and prevent distractions. Emphasize the importance of digital detoxing. Discuss the benefits of taking intentional breaks from digital devices to reduce distractions and enhance one's ability to be fully present.

Discuss the concept of mindful eating. Encourage savoring each bite, paying attention to flavors and textures, and fostering a deeper connection with the act of nourishing oneself. Encourage observation of the surroundings. Discuss the value of being present by actively observing and appreciating the details of the environment, whether indoors or outdoors. Highlight sensory engagement. Encourage individuals to engage their senses fully, whether through listening to soothing music, feeling textures, enjoying scents, or relishing the taste of food. Discuss the incorporation of hygge-inspired rituals.

Encourage the establishment of daily rituals, such as morning routines, tea or coffee breaks, or evening rituals, that promote a sense of presence and calm. Emphasize the power of pauses. Discuss the idea of incorporating short pauses throughout the day to reflect, breathe, and refocus, allowing individuals to reset and be fully present.

Discuss the benefits of single-tasking. Encourage the practice of focusing on one task at a time, promoting efficiency, reduced stress, and a deeper connection with the activity. Encourage the creation of mindfulness spaces.

Discuss the concept of setting up dedicated spaces at home—whether a cozy nook or a quiet corner—where individuals can retreat to practice mindfulness. Discuss the role of gratitude in being present.

Encourage the daily practice of acknowledging and expressing gratitude, fostering a positive mindset and awareness of the blessings in one's life. Highlight mindful technology practices. Discuss the importance of using technology with intention, setting boundaries, and being aware of the impact of digital interactions on one's present state. Discuss engaging in mindful movement.

Encourage activities like yoga, tai chi, or gentle stretching exercises that promote mindful movement, connecting the body and mind in the present moment. Emphasize the art of mindful listening. Discuss the practice of fully engaging in conversations by listening attentively, being present, and fostering deeper connections with others. Discuss the mindful approach to leisure. Encourage individuals to approach leisure activities with mindfulness, whether it's reading a book, enjoying a hobby, or simply resting and being present in the moment. Highlight setting daily intentions. Discuss the practice of starting each day with a clear intention, guiding individuals to approach their activities with purpose and awareness. Encourage mindful journaling. Discuss the benefits of journaling as a reflective practice, providing individuals with a tool to express thoughts, emotions, and moments of gratitude. Discuss the availability of mindfulness courses. Encourage individuals to explore online or community-based mindfulness courses that offer guidance and practices for cultivating presence in daily life.

Conclusion

The hygge lifestyle is not just a trend but a timeless philosophy that invites individuals to embrace simplicity, cultivate warmth, and cherish the present moment. As we conclude this exploration into the world of hygge, let's reflect on the key principles and practices that can guide us towards a cozier and meaningful existence.

Hygge is not merely a set of practices; it's a mindset that prioritizes comfort, connection, and appreciation for life's simple pleasures. By adopting this mindset, individuals can create spaces and moments that radiate warmth and contentment.

A central theme of hygge is the emphasis on connection and togetherness. Whether it's sharing a meal with loved ones, engaging in heartfelt conversations, or simply being present with friends and family, the sense of community contributes significantly to a hygge lifestyle.

Mindful technology use is crucial in the hygge lifestyle. Taking breaks from screens, being present in face-to-face interactions, and creating digital detox moments contribute to a more balanced and intentional approach to technology.

Hygge encourages a connection to nature, and this extends to home decor. Integrating natural elements, such as plants, wooden accents, and earthy color palettes, brings a touch of the outdoors inside, creating a harmonious and comforting living space.

The concept of being present, whether through mindful breathing, focused attention, or gratitude practices, is fundamental to hygge.

By incorporating these mindful practices into daily life, individuals can enhance their overall well-being and find joy in the simplicity of each moment.

Extending hygge principles to the workplace promotes a more relaxed and collaborative atmosphere. Simple gestures like bringing a mug to work, decorating the workspace, and fostering teamwork contribute to a more hygge-inspired work environment. Cozy home spaces are at the heart of hygge. From soft textures and warm lighting to personalized decor and comfortable seating, creating a hygge-inspired environment involves curating spaces that invite relaxation and a sense of sanctuary. Hygge is not reserved for special occasions—it's a lifestyle woven into everyday moments. Whether it's setting a hygge-inspired table, taking a mindful walk, or embracing the small joys of life, integrating these rituals enhances the overall hygge experience.

As we navigate the complexities of modern life, the hygge philosophy serves as a gentle reminder to slow down, savor the present, and surround ourselves with the warmth and comfort that truly matter. By incorporating hygge into our lives, we embark on a journey towards a more intentional, connected, and joyous way of living. May your days be filled with hygge, and may you find contentment in the simplicity of each moment.

Thank you, and good luck!

Resources

https://www.telegraph.co.uk/travel/discovering-hygge-in-copenhagen/eight-ways-to-be-happier/
https://www.ftd.com/blog/share/hygge-decor-ideas
https://www.housebeautiful.com/uk/lifestyle/news/a2618/ways-to-create-hygge-happiness-at-home/
https://www.mentalfloss.com/article/91378/10-ways-master-danish-art-hygge-your-home
https://alternativemindset.net/7-ideas-elevate-backyard-ho-hum-hygge-haven/
https://www.perrywood.co.uk/gardening-tips/five-ways-bring-hygge-garden/
https://www.sunset.com/home-garden/outdoor-living/hygge-home#guitar-players-campfire
https://www.housebeautiful.com/uk/garden/a870/7-ways-to-bring-hygge-to-your-garden/
https://www.thompson-morgan.com/gardening-articles/how-to-hygge-your-garden
https://www.verywellmind.com/health-benefits-of-hygge-4164281
https://www.countryliving.com/life/a41187/what-is-hygge-things-to-know-about-the-danish-lifestyle-trend/
https://www.ftd.com/blog/share/hygge-decor-ideas
https://www.birchbox.com/magazine/article/how-to-embrace-hygge-the-danish-lifestyle-concept
https://abeautifulmess.com/2020/03/how-to-Hygge.html
https://www.businessnewsdaily.com/9983-hygge-at-work.html

Made in United States
Orlando, FL
13 May 2024